Focused Observations

Focused Observations

How to Observe Children for Assessment and Curriculum Planning

> Gaye Gronlund and Marlyn James

Redleaf Press®
www.redleafpress.org
800-423-8309

Published by Redleaf Press
10 Yorkton Court
St. Paul, MN 55117
www.redleafpress.org

Photos by Steve Wewerka
Interior typeset in LinoLetter Roman and designed by Cathy Spengler Design
Printed in the United States of America
17 16 15 14 13 12 11 10   5 6 7 8 9 10 11 12

Library of Congress Cataloging-in-Publication Data

Gronlund, Gaye, 1952–
    Focused observations : how to observe children for assessment and
curriculum planning / Gaye Gronlund and Marlyn James.
        p. cm.
    ISBN 978-1-929610-71-6
1. Observation (Educational method) 2. Educational tests and measurement.
3. Early childhood education. 4. Curriculum planning. I. James, Marlyn. II. Title.

LB1027.28.G76 2005
372.1102—dc22

                            2005013478

Printed on acid-free paper

Gaye: *To Bruce, with all my love*

Marlyn: *To my husband and life partner, Chuck, for his ever-present support and encouragement. And in memory of my dad for giving me the courage of my convictions and for always asking me "why?"*

From both of us: *to Betty Jones, Laila Aaen, and Louise Derman-Sparks. You all inspired us to make the most of our Pacific Oaks experiences, both as students and as faculty. Thank you for all of your contributions to our thinking and understanding about early childhood practices.*

Contents

Acknowledgments

Many thanks to the following people:

- Diana Lamb, Teacher/Director, and the families at Little Lamb Nursery School, Lebanon, Indiana
- Dawn Blake, Director, and all of the staff and families at Epworth Weekday Children's Ministries, Indianapolis, Indiana
- Special thanks to the following teachers at Epworth for sharing their comments:
    - Darlisa Davis
    - Johanna Schaub
    - Robin Jones
    - Pam Berg
- Ted Maple, Director, and all of the staff and families at St. Mary's Child Center, Indianapolis, Indiana
- Ken Scheidler of Anthology Video, Indianapolis, Indiana
- Peggy Seaman, A Joyful Noise Family Child Care Home, Columbia Falls, Montana
- Collette Box, Director, Discovery Developmental Center, Kalispell, Montana
- Mary Lyons, The Nurturing Center, Kalispell, Montana
- All of the teachers and families of the New Mexico Office of Child Development Focused Portfolios Project
- Students in the Early Childhood Education Program at Flathead Valley Community College, Kalispell, Montana
- And our editor, Beth Wallace

Introduction

Have you or your colleagues ever made a statement like this one?
"I observe my children all day, but I don't have time to write down what I'm seeing. That takes me away from the kids. And they just need me too much."

Sound familiar? In our work as college instructors and consultants, we've heard variations on this comment many, many times. And we recognize how true it is! Your job is demanding and your time limited. If you are expected to observe and write down your observations, you can easily feel overwhelmed and frustrated.

That's why we wrote this book. We wanted to give practical explanations of how to observe children in order to assess their development and plan curriculum. We wanted to offer a comprehensive and user-friendly source with realistic ideas of how to put observation into practice. We wanted to offer lots of observation notes and an accompanying set of video vignettes of children in action so that you could get better at observing children and writing down what you see. Our goal is to help early educators recognize the importance of observation and learn ways to fit it into a busy day with children.

From our experiences as teachers ourselves, as well as our work with early educators all over the country, we have learned that being a good observer makes working with children easier and more satisfying in the long run. When teachers observe children, they get to know them better. They can provide the right challenges and support; they can see trouble coming and head it off. It seems like more work—it *is* more work—but it will ultimately make your job easier.

We have included many different ways for you to practice and refine your observation skills. You can try out various ways of writing your observations down. You can experiment with using what you learn about the children through observing them. And, through practice, you can figure out your own style of doing observation well. No two observers are the same. Each will bring to the experience her own personality, her own educational and cultural background, and her own life experiences.

This book and video are designed to go hand in hand. At the end of every chapter video vignettes are identified, and activities are suggested. These video activities can be used in college course work, staff development sessions, in-service workshops, and staff meetings. Our suggestion is that you read the chapter before viewing the video vignettes and doing the activities. In this way you come to the video experience with basic knowledge and suggestions to apply to the viewing.

The book can also be used without the video. At the end of every chapter are suggested activities to help you practice observation in your own work or family setting. Applying what you read, trying it out for yourself, analyzing what worked and didn't work, and reflecting on what you learned through the observation experience can be done with the video vignettes or in your own life settings. It's the practice that is the most important!

For each activity we have identified a purpose, a suggested video vignette or a situation to observe, the process for watching the child and documenting what is seen, and a focus for group discussion. The activities correlate with the order of the video vignettes from number one through number sixteen. However, you can use each practice observation in many different ways. Watching the same video vignette more than once will increase your understanding of how much can be learned through observation and give you more in-depth knowledge of ways to interpret what is seen.

In addition to the video activities, two other types of activities are included at the end of each chapter:

■ Reflection
■ Finding Your Observation Style

The reflection activities are designed to help you think about the content of the chapter, analyzing and applying that content to your experiences with observation of children. You can answer the questions in written form as a formal assignment, or you can use them for discussion starters. The second set of activities, Finding Your Observation Style, is designed to be used in an ongoing journal format. We hope that by keeping a personal journal about your trials and errors with observation, you will discover your own strengths and weaknesses in observing children. We also hope that by the end of your experience with this book and video, you will think differently about the comment we shared at the beginning of this Introduction.

The next time you hear someone say, "I observe my children all day, but I don't have time to write down what I'm seeing. That takes me away from the kids. And they just need me too much," we hope you'll answer, "Yes, observation and documentation are hard work. But it's worth it! Now I make time for it because I see how much I learn about the children!"

chapter 1

Date Feb. 10 (may be us

Art

11 mins

nipulatives

Science/Math

mins.

Music/Movemen

O

O

Why Observe Children?

By observing children you get to know them better and are more in tune with their needs and personalities. Knowing children better makes caring for them much easier. You are more able to head off trouble before it arises if you watch for the initial signals of an oncoming meltdown or a brewing confrontation between two children. You can observe and sense when you need to help a three-year-old who is getting frustrated putting together a difficult puzzle, or a nine-month-old who has just started crawling and tends to get stuck when trying to get around objects in his way. You become aware of how a child copes with separation from her family members, and can be ready to help her. You learn how each child uniquely expresses his creativity and offer him materials to do so.

Your observations provide a fuller, richer picture of each child so that your curriculum planning can address the specific capabilities of the children in your care. Activities you plan will be more successful for you and the children. Because you will be aware of their strengths, weaknesses, interests, and passions, you will choose materials and projects that engage them for longer periods of time. Then you will be able to observe them even more because they stay with the activity that much longer!

You naturally observe children any time you care for them. If you are a parent caring for your baby, or an aunt taking care of a niece or nephew, you note what the baby's general mood is and make decisions based on what you see and hear. If the baby is smiling and cooing, you may smile and coo back. You may feel reassured that you don't need to do anything else right then. If the baby is crying and fussy, you may try a variety of strategies to settle the baby down—including changing a diaper, offering a pacifier, picking the baby up and talking softly and gently to her, or heating up a bottle for a feeding. All of these actions are based on your observations of the child's signals and cues, the child's behavior, and his ways of communicating his needs.

You do the same when caring for preschool-aged children in your family. You listen to the children and watch their behavior carefully in order to determine how best to take care of the routines of the day, to help them learn and grow, and to help them gain self-control and develop independence. Through their observations, caring parents and relatives develop an intimacy with children and a deep knowledge of their personalities, temperaments, and capabilities.

When you care for children in a child care setting or a preschool, you also naturally observe them. Observations help you to determine not only what needs the child has but also how you can be a more effective teacher for him. When a new child begins in your program, you plan ways to get to know her. Observing her in action with adults, with other children, and by herself helps you learn just who this child is and what she can do. Observations also guide you in determining the next steps to take with the child in order to support her growth and help her progress to her fullest potential.

In this book we help you learn how to focus your observations. In addition, we share ways for you to systematically document or record what you learn about children through observation. Throughout the chapters we include observation notes of children in action so that you can review them and learn more about children's development, see different ways of recording information, and draw conclusions about curricular strategies. We also share comments we heard in interviews with

Johanna: *After you've been doing observations for a while, you start to find the joy in it, because the children push themselves and you start to realize, "Wow, this is really neat to see what they want to learn."*

early educators using observation. We hope that you will learn practical tips and helpful recommendations from their experiences. Activities at the end of each chapter help you apply what you learn. If you have the video that accompanies this book, you will be asked to watch the vignettes and use them as discussion starters and practice sessions. If you do not have access to the video, we will give you suggestions for observing children in your work or home setting so that you can have the same opportunities for practice.

Spontaneous or Planned Observation

Your observations can be spontaneous in nature. Sometimes you take in information as it happens and add it to your internal thinking about each child. In these instances, you are truly in the moment with children and are enjoying the interactions to their fullest. Many teachers report that there is nothing as delightful as witnessing the sense of accomplishment when a child tries something new and, with bright eyes and a big grin, announces, "I did it!" Being there to smile with the child, to offer a hug and say "Congratulations!" is very rewarding.

Your observations can also be planned and documented. In order to truly get to know each child and to be ready to figure out the best ways to help him, planned observations are necessary. They help you to make sure that no area of development or daily experience is missed. And documentation—writing the observation down—is essential in order to remember clearly what each child can do and how each one responds to different situations. The documentation is an ongoing record to help you reflect about each child. And that documentation of your observation provides you with evidence to share and reflect upon with the child's family members or with other specialists if necessary. Documentation can also help you explain what you are doing to help children learn and grow, so that families understand more about your curriculum. Parents say that when teachers share observations of their children at play, they understand more about the value of play and exploration. Teachers report that these parents then offer more support for what goes on in the program. Your observations open a window onto the world of their children during their time with you and invite family members to share more fully in their children's experiences away from home.

Beata: *When you share your observations with parents, they see that you are really concentrating on their child. They see that they're doing work. It's not that they just play or that they're just wandering around the classroom. They see that you're really focused on them.*

Two Ways for You to Use Observation Information

You gain lots of information by observing children. There are two primary ways for you to use that information:

- For assessment
- For curriculum planning

The two are intricately woven together. You observe children to learn more about who they are and what they can do so that you can more effectively plan activities, choose materials, offer adult guidance, and encourage peer interactions that support the child's growth and development. As you implement your plan for activities, materials, and interactions, you observe again to see how successfully your plan meets the child's needs. You assess that success and plan again! The process is ongoing.

Observing to Assess a Child

Assessing a child does not mean the same thing as testing a child. Assessment is a process of gathering information about a child's capabilities. It may be done through observation, through collection of work samples or photographs, through parent interviews, and through tests. Once the information is gathered, you have evidence to evaluate the child's skill levels, strengths, weaknesses, personality traits, and interests. Using a combination of the processes listed above helps you make an informed judgment about a child's progress and her approaches to learning (Council for Chief State School Officers 2003).

Observing children for assessment purposes can be done in a spontaneous way without writing down what you see or in a more systematic and thoughtful manner with careful planning for documentation. The problem with informal, undocumented observation is that the assessment evidence is all in the teacher's mind. There is no record for you or for others to follow that documents the child's changes over time, the child's progress, the child's struggles, the interventions teachers have attempted, and the results of those interventions. With no record of observations, bias and prejudice may go unrecognized and influence decisions about the child. Keeping the assessment process as only an internal one is not recommended by early childhood professional organizations.

Informal observation is more valuable for assessment when joined with more formal, planned, and documented observation. With written records of things witnessed, of what children said and did, you can build a case about each child. You can share this evidence with others, using it to support your conclusions about the child's development. Formal, planned, and documented observation helps you make sure no child is missed, no area of development is neglected, and appropriate next steps are planned.

When observing to assess a child's development, you can think in broad terms, trying to understand the child's cognitive stage of development (as based on the work of Jean Piaget and Lev Vygotsky, for example) or his general competencies in the social and emotional areas (as based on the work of Erik Erikson, for example). Or you can observe for instances in which the child shows his specific skills and capabilities. These specific observations can then be tied to developmental checklists that include cognitive, physical, social, and emotional information for specific age groups. By turning to such sources to evaluate your observations, you are comparing the child's performance to reasonable expectations for children her age. Choosing reputable and respected sources for such information is a crucial part of the process. In Chapter 4 we discuss in depth how to observe to assess these broad stages and specific skills and share various developmental checklists and resources.

Observing to Plan Curriculum

The purpose of observing and identifying children's developmental capabilities is not for accountability or reporting purposes alone. It also helps you plan curriculum that meets the child's needs. Identifying a child's present performance gives you a place to start, a baseline. Then you take the all-important step of deciding what materials, activities, adult interactions, and peer involvement will be most effective in meeting each child's present level of performance and supporting her movement toward higher-level skills and capabilities.

Observing with curriculum in mind can be spontaneous and informal, or more focused and planned. You may respond automatically to a child's request for a different material or immediately act upon your realization that more chairs are needed around the playdough table. You may lift an infant out of his seat as you notice his beginning agitation

Pam: *In my class of five-year-olds, since I started observing, I'm more in line with what my kids are doing in the classroom. And, therefore, I'm ready to change when they're ready to change instead of when I'm ready to change. For example, by watching how they're cutting, I can keep a more precise count on how many kids in my class can cut correctly. Or I can observe how many kids in my class are reading most of the time. And I can now change my teaching based on that.*

and carry him across the room so that he can see what the other children are doing. These are all spontaneous curricular decisions. You are responding to something you have seen and making changes in materials, environment, or interaction with the child.

Being more focused and planned may involve identifying areas of the classroom to observe more closely. You may see parts of the play area that are hardly used by the children, while other areas are overcrowded. Room rearrangement may be necessary to help with traffic flow. Or you may notice that the toddlers are especially fascinated with the fish in the aquarium this week. Figuring out ways to follow up on their interest will help you be responsive to the children and develop their engagement and understanding. Sometimes you may need to communicate with your colleagues to decide who will observe specific activities or watch for the children's demonstration of certain skills. Some teaching teams will plan ahead to watch for children's evidence of their fine motor skills and will put out a variety of stringing beads and pegs and pegboards so that they can collect information related to that area. Determining goals for the observation will help you collect information that can contribute to a later discussion or a change in plans. And documenting, or writing down what you notice as you observe an activity or area, will help you remember more clearly what was seen and make more effective decisions for change. In Chapter 5 we will offer more in-depth suggestions about using observation for curriculum planning.

What Can You Learn by Observing Children?

Whether you are observing children for assessment or curriculum planning purposes, you learn more about them. You learn about all these facets of the whole child:

- Their developmental capabilities in all areas: social, emotional, physical, and cognitive
- Their personalities
- How they cope with difficult situations and solve problems
- What might be behind their behavior
- Their deep interests and passions
- The information and knowledge they are constructing
- Their expression of their cultural backgrounds

Observation gives a thorough, well-rounded picture of what is important to know about children.

Pam: *This was my sixth year of teaching preschool, and I feel like I know my kids so much better than I ever have before because I'm watching them more closely. I'm paying attention to the little things they're doing.*

On the following pages are several observation notes that illustrate each of the possibilities of what can be learned (see above list). After each note we show how you can use the information gained from that observation to assess the child's development and to plan curriculum accordingly.

Learning about Children's Developmental Capabilities

Observing a child's participation in daily routines, play, and activities is a way to collect facts about his developmental capabilities. Think about all of the developmental areas that are possible to observe during a daily routine such as snack. The potential for seeing development in action is limitless. Practice by analyzing the following observation note about Angel. This observation took place over a short time period (a few minutes at most). As you read the note, write down the areas of development (cognitive, physical, social, and emotional) covered by this observation.

> Angel (4 yrs. 10 mos.)
At snack Angel saved a chair and called to his friend Luis, "You sit here next to me!" He took three crackers, counting out, "One, two, three," as he put them on his napkin. He used a knife to spread peanut butter across each one. When he wanted more juice, he called out, "More juice, please!" In conversation with his friends he said, "At our farm we have chickens and goats. And the goats are very loud. I have to cover my ears because they are so loud." Angel covered his ears with two napkins, and his friend Luis did the same, but Luis used his crackers. Both boys laughed.

Here is a list of Angel's capabilities organized into the major areas, or domains, of child development. You can see that every major area was contained in this short observation.

- Cognitive development: counting to three with one-to-one correspondence, figuring out to cover his ears with his napkin, using language to ask for more and to express his life experiences
- Physical development: sitting on a chair at a table, spreading peanut butter with a knife
- Social development: asking his friend to sit with him
- Emotional development: talking with and enjoying his friend

Using information for assessment Assessing Angel's capabilities means relating his actions to what you know about children his age. Turning to developmental checklists or other sources of information, you could determine that Angel is functioning right at age level in his social interactions with his friend, his use of language to express himself, and his ability to use his fine motor skills to spread with a knife. You may note that counting to three with one-to-one correspondence is at the level of a younger child. You would expect an almost-five-year-old to count a higher quantity of objects.

Using information for planning You may decide that in the areas of social, language, and physical capabilities all that you and your colleagues need to do is to support Angel. In the cognitive area as demonstrated by his counting, you may decide to do some specific counting activities to see if Angel can indeed count higher quantities of objects and maintain the one-to-one correspondence. You may offer him many opportunities to play with and count manipulatives, to count the children in the room, and to count as he jumps on a trampoline or swings on a swing outside.

Learning about Children's Personalities

When observing children, you can see their personalities in action and identify ways each child functions in the world. Using this information helps you support each child's integration into the community of your classroom. Read the following observation note about Kassandra and write down what you are learning about her personality.

> Kassandra (3 yrs. 11 mos.)
> Kassandra has been absent for a few days, and when she comes into the classroom, she goes up to her teacher and says, "Hello! I'm back! Did you miss me?" The teacher replies, "Yes, I did! And I'm so happy to see you back and feeling better." Kassandra then goes up to one of her peers and says, "Hello. See, I'm back, and I'm not crying. Let's go play!"

Using information for assessment You can see that Kassandra has a positive sense of self. The egocentricity (or self-centered nature) of an almost-four-year-old is evident, as is her confidence in her teacher's and friend's concern for her. She uses language to express herself well. You could refer to developmental checklists to help you recognize that the skills she demonstrates in this observation are at her age level.

Using information for planning You may have a history with Kassandra and know that she has had problems in the past with feeling sad and crying when she arrived at your program, especially after being absent for a few days. Here you can recognize that she is adjusting to being back in the classroom with smiles and no tears. Giving her a hug or patting her on the back and telling her how you are noticing her growth and self-confidence will encourage her to continue to separate from her family members more easily. You can tell her mother at pickup time what happened in the morning so that she can celebrate Kassandra's progress in separating with no tears as well. If Kassandra does have a hard day again in the future, you can remind her of this day and her success or offer that she draw or paint how she is feeling to help her express herself in other ways.

Learning about How Children Cope with Difficult Situations

When we care for children, we often see how they cope with the ins and outs of difficult times throughout the day. Getting along in a group setting is hard work for them and involves developing problem-solving skills. Read the following observation note about Corlyn and write down what you see her strategies are to find comfort when she is upset.

> Corlyn (1 yr. 3 mos.)
> When Corlyn begins to be tired and starts to cry after eating lunch, she will walk to her cubby and reach for her diaper bag. She will look in the side pocket for her pacifier. If it's in that pocket, she will take it out and stick it in her mouth. Then she will find her blanket on her mat and go to sleep.

Using information for assessment Corlyn independently seeks out her pacifier to comfort herself. She knows where it's located and shows initiative to get it. She shows excellent skills in coping with difficulties for her age level.

Using information for planning Anticipating Corlyn's difficult time after lunch and having her pacifier or a stuffed animal nearby would prevent her initial crying. Praising her when she does get it herself with positive words and a quick hug would help her settle down into naptime with adult comfort as well.

Insight into Children's Behavior

Observation can provide insight into a child's behavior, whether positive or negative. Many children like Ansen in the following observation note are trying hard to learn appropriate ways to get their needs met. But often they become frustrated and communicate through hitting or other physical means and need a teacher's help to negotiate with other children. Read the following observation note about Ansen and write down what you are learning about his behavior.

> Ansen (4 yrs. 10 mos.)
> Ansen is playing on the hanging bars. A child is hanging upside down. Ansen asks, "When will you be done? I have been waiting a long time." The child does not respond. Ansen waits a few more minutes, and then attempts to hit the child in the head. A teacher walks over and asks why he has a fist. Ansen replies, "I want a turn, and Kristen won't get down. She stuck her tongue out at me." "Is there a better way to get a turn?" asks the teacher. Ansen says, "I used my words, and she won't listen. She wants it all to herself." The teacher asks the child to listen to Ansen. Ansen says, "I want a turn when you're done. I won't hit you. But you listen." The teacher talks to both children, and they continue playing on the bars.

Using information for assessment Ansen does not quite have the self-control to stop himself from hitting another child when frustrated. Yet he does use words to express his feelings and is successful in resolving the problem once an adult helps him talk with the other child. Resolving such disagreements with adult help is common for children his age.

Using information for planning Ansen will still need adults nearby and ready to step in and prevent him from harming other children and helping him work out disagreements more appropriately. You and your colleagues might decide to always have someone keeping an eye on him to be ready to provide that support. When he does resolve disagreements peacefully, you will praise his use of words, giving him pats on the back or high fives to reward his hard work.

Learning about Children's Deep Interests and Passions

Observation helps you see what children's interests are. Noting what areas of the classroom they spend time in or what materials they choose to use again and again gives you insight into their strengths and comforts. Paying attention to the topics that they talk about or incorporate into their play can help you plan curriculum that will be based on their interests and be more motivating to them. Read the following observation note about Darius and Justin. Notice how they show their interest in cooking and write down follow-up activities that you would plan for these boys both indoors and outdoors to continue to build on that interest.

> Darius (4 yrs. 5 mos.), Justin (4 yrs. 8 mos.)
> Darius and Justin go to play in the sandbox after a cooking project. Darius says to Justin, "Let's make what Antonio's mom makes. Pass the sugar. That's 1 cup of teaspoon. We crack the eggs. We need milk, cinnamon, need teaspoon salt." He uses a shovel to add sand to the measuring cup. He takes the cup and pours it into the bowl. He takes a spoon and adds more sand, and then moves the spoon around in the bowl. He pours it onto a plate and tells Justin, "Okay. Take it to the oven."

Using information for assessment Both boys are playing out cooking steps that they experienced in classroom cooking activities. Such representation of real objects with sand shows their abstract thinking and ability to pretend, all-important cognitive capabilities for children their age.

Using information for planning Inviting Darius and Justin to help prepare snack foods, to write out simple recipes, to plan future cooking activities, and to use measuring cups and spoons in sand and water outdoors would all be ways of using this observation for curriculum planning purposes.

Learning about the Information and Knowledge Children Are Constructing

Through their play and use of materials, children often show you what information and knowledge they are figuring out and what skills they are working on. Read the following note about Fernando and identify what knowledge and skills he is showing in this observation.

> Fernando (3 yrs. 7 mos.)
> While drawing at the art table, Fernando uses different colored markers. When he is finished, I ask him to tell me about his picture. He points to the large, yellow circle and says it is a big animal. Then he says, "This is purple, and this is red." Fernando then gets a purple marker and draws the letter "F" in the left-hand corner. He says, "F for Fernando."

Using information for assessment Fernando is showing his beginning literacy and fine motor skills as he draws a circle and a letter "F," all advanced skills for his age. He also is showing his growing vocabulary and understanding of concepts by identifying colors.

Using information for planning Fernando may enjoy working with a name card so that he can see the other letters in his name and attempt to represent them. To help him continue to develop the muscles in his hand for writing, you could provide him with opportunities to work with playdough, string beads, build with small connecting blocks, and draw and write with markers. Offering him opportunities to match and label colored objects will help build his vocabulary of color words.

Learning about Children's Expression of Their Cultural Backgrounds

Children's cultural backgrounds show through in their play and the ways that they function in everyday routines as well. Sometimes teachers' assumptions about how a child should go about eating or toileting are different from a family's assumptions. Whether this difference is due to culture, class, or another factor, to serve the child well, teachers have to understand the difference to begin with. Read this note about Yuta, and note the difference between the early educators' assumptions and the child's and family's expectations.

> Yuta (1 yr. 8 mos.)
> Every day Yuta sits in his high chair waiting to be fed. We wonder why he will not begin to eat the food that is placed on his high chair. The only way he eats is if we feed him.

Using information for assessment and planning In this case, the teachers involved decided that they needed more information in order to understand Yuta's behavior around eating. Here is what the teacher says about what this team did:

> *After talking with the family we learned that it was typical for Japanese families to feed their children for a long time, not stopping completely until the child starts grade school. We had to deal with our assumptions and accept that this was a part of this family's culture. We now feed Yuta each day.*

Observation can provide you with a wealth of information about children. You decide how best to use that information to be a better teacher, to understand a child's behavior more fully, and to communicate with others about what you are learning.

Finding Your Observation Style

Implementing observation is a process that may look different from one teacher to another, from one care setting to another. Finding your unique style of watching children in action—figuring out when to write down your observations, how to file and organize those records, and how to evaluate them and present them to parents—is an important part of developing your own professionalism. Throughout this book you will be offered many ideas, tips, and strategies based on early childhood professionals' experiences with observation. These ideas will help you find your unique observation style and make it successful for you in your work with young children and families.

Observation Practice: What Can You Learn?

Purpose: To identify what can be learned by observing a child for a brief period of time in a daily routine

What to Do: If you have access to the *Focused Observations* video, watch Vignette 1, "Washing Hands and Snack," which shows Daniel (4 yrs. 2 mos.). Watch Daniel in the video go through the daily routines associated with snack time. As you watch, make note of all the things you see that Daniel can do. If you do not have the *Focused Observations* video, observe a child you know during a daily routine, and make note of all the things you see that the child can do.

Group Discussion: Generate a list of Daniel's capabilities, skills, social interactions, personality traits, and behaviors, or those of the child you know if you are not using the video. Be prepared to share this list with others, and discuss these questions:

   ■ Were you surprised at how much you learned in a short observation?

   ■ If you watched the video: If you had a history with Daniel, would you have seen things differently? In what ways?

   ■ If you observed a child you know: Did knowing the child enable you to see something in a new or different light? Why or why not?

   ■ What curriculum plans might you make based on what you learned?

Reflection

Purpose: To reflect how observation affects adults' relationships with children

What to Do: Think about a time in your life when you learned something special about a child. Then discuss or write about these questions:

   ■ What factors were present that allowed you to learn about this child?

   ■ Did observing the child contribute to your learning about him or her? In what situations did you observe this child?

   ■ How did the relationship change as you got to know the child better?

   ■ Did learning about the child help you to understand the child's motivations?

Think about an adult who knew you well when you were a child. Then respond to these questions:

   ■ How did that person come to know you well?

   ■ What factors were present that allowed the adult to get to know you?

- Do you think that observation contributed to this person's learning about you? In what situations were you observed?
- How did you feel as a child knowing that this person knew you well and understood you?

Finding Your Observation Style

Purpose: To discover what you already know about observation, and what you want to learn more about

What to Do: Begin an ongoing journal in which you record your answers to questions posed throughout this book. Here are some questions to get you started. Spend a few minutes jotting down your responses to them.

- What do you already know about observation? Do you observe children in your work and life? What do you think you learn by observing children?
- Do you tend to observe for one area of development (cognitive, physical, social, or emotional) more than another? Which one is more dominant in your observations? Which area do you tend to watch the least?
- What are some questions you have about observation? What do you want to learn more about?

References

- Council for Chief State School Officers Early Childhood Education Assessment Panel. 2003. The words we use: A glossary of terms for early childhood education standards and assessment. http://www.ccsso.org.

chapter 2

Preschool Cho

Date Feb. 10

(may be used to tally one child's choi

Child(ren)

Art	
	Social/Emot
11 mins	

nipulatives

mins.

0

How Do You Do Observation Well?

When you start out observing children, you may feel overwhelmed by the amount of information you are seeing. You may struggle with where to focus your attention and just what to write down. You may miss children or areas of development. You may find certain areas of the classroom easier to pay attention to than others. Some children may demand your attention and are easy to focus on, while others seem to slip under the radar. But you can work on your observation skills, get better over time, and feel successful. Over time you can learn to do observation well by doing the following:

- Choosing a focus for your observations
- Using all of your senses to observe
- Giving yourself time to practice observation
- Becoming open and ready for children
- Thinking of observation as research
- Giving yourself time to reflect about your observations
- Becoming aware of your own biases

■ Documenting factually

■ Working hard not to miss any children

Focusing Observations

Observing children can be overwhelming. Figuring out ways to focus your observations will lessen the amount of information coming in and help you determine where to turn your attention. Sometimes your focus will be more general in nature, and other times more specific. Here are some specific things you might choose to focus on:

■ You can focus on the moment with the child.

■ You can focus on a group of children.

■ You can focus on specific daily routines, activities, or areas of the classroom.

■ You can focus on skills or areas of development (such as fine motor skills or early literacy understanding).

■ You can focus on challenges for each child and identify teaching strategies to help address those challenges.

Allowing yourself the freedom to move back and forth among different perspectives will help you juggle the demands of the classroom and still be a competent observer.

You cannot possibly write down everything that you have seen the children do in a day. Documenting your observations involves some decision making on your part. You will want to choose a focus for the observations that you will write down. You and your colleagues may divide up observation and documentation to help make the best use of your time. In this book we give you all sorts of tips and strategies so that you can figure out the best ways to document observations when you are in the midst of running a busy classroom. In Chapter 3 we help you figure out the best times to observe and introduce you to many different methods of recording observations. In Chapter 4 we suggest ideas to help you observe specifically for assessment purposes. And in Chapter 5 we offer ideas to help observe for curriculum planning.

Observing with All of Your Senses

Early educators do not observe with their eyes alone. They observe with most of their senses: sight, hearing, touch, smell. Seeing is the most obvious way to observe what children do. Being a good observer involves using your eyes to scan the room, taking in the big picture

Robin: *The reality in this field is that we don't get paid a lot of money. And we don't have a lot of time to do observation and documentation as well as they need to be done. And so, if you can view it almost as a labor of love and just shift your attitude to know why you're doing this . . . because it helps you become a better teacher. Keeping my attitude focused and being able to force myself to do these observations in a more focused way help me to pick up where I drop the ball sometimes. My class is more well rounded.*

of what all of the children are doing, as well as focusing in and really watching what individual children are doing. But seeing cannot stand alone in observing the intricacies of each child's performance.

Think of a time when you were with a child or a group of children, and you had to look away for a minute. Perhaps you had to turn your back in order to take some materials off a shelf. Would you say that you were still observing your children? Of course you were! That's because you were listening.

Taking in information by listening is a critical part of the observation process. Hearing a baby's cries or coos and responding appropriately help to make sure that baby learns to trust her caregivers and knows that she will be well taken care of. Listening to a child's story of his visit to Grandma's house validates his experience and encourages his communication with others. Listening to a child's wheezing cough raises concerns about her health and might lead to calling her family so they can take her to the clinic. Listening to an infant's calm breathing assures you that naptime is going smoothly. Sometimes even knowing when things have gotten too quiet in one part of the classroom is a form of observation and may cause you to check out what might be going on with the children there.

Sense of touch is an important part of the observation process as well. Early childhood teachers often touch children as a way of building relationships with them. Babies are held so that the caregiver can be close to the child's range of vision and provide the stimulation and nurturing that are so important. Toddlers explore their independence and return to the safe haven of their favorite teacher's loving arms. For toddlers and preschoolers, a pat on the back, a handshake, a high five, and a hug are ways to say "Hello," to recognize a job well done, or to comfort a hurt feeling or an injury. Inviting children to sit on laps is often part of reading stories in a small or large group time. An adult's lap often provides a sense of security to a child who is missing Mom or Dad or helps a child who does not have control of his own body to settle down and participate more appropriately in the activity.

Sensitive care providers recognize that each child has her own comfort levels with touch. Some children welcome affection and often initiate it themselves. Others have a stronger sense of personal space and bristle or withdraw from too invasive a gesture from an adult. This can be especially true in the early days of a relationship, but some children are less open to touch in general. There are cultural differences regarding physical interaction among people, as well. In some cultures adults carry the children longer into their preschool years than in others. The accepted distance between two people when talking also varies from culture to culture. Some people are comfortable being very close when communicating, while others prefer more distance. Becoming aware of the cultural preferences of the children and families in your program will help you interpret more accurately as you observe through physical contact and touch.

An alert teacher can watch carefully for the signals a child is sending through the child's response to touch. You can also read the child's body language through your own sense of touch. Is the baby you are holding squirming and agitated? Or is he nestled against you, relaxed and restful? Is the child sitting on your lap rigid and stiff when hugged? Does she hug back or withdraw slightly? Paying attention to physical cues is an important part of observation.

Sense of smell is also useful in observing children. For babies and toddlers, especially, and sometimes with preschoolers as well, teachers' sense of smell is important regarding changing diapers or handling toileting accidents. Concerns about children's hygiene can be identified through sense of smell. Making referrals to administrators and outside agencies when children are unkempt and not bathed may be the start of some helpful intervention for a family. And identifying health concerns for children often begins with smells. When a child arrives at school with a stuffed-up nose, breathing through his mouth, you may note the smell of his breath and recognize that an infection may be developing in his throat. Alerting a family member that medical attention is needed is an important part of communication about a child's care.

Finally, dedicated teachers observe with their hearts. As you get to know your children, and you build a strong relationship based on your observations and interactions with each child, you can "see" with your heart when something is not right for a child. You may find yourself saying something like, "She just wasn't herself today." Then you can ask the parents if anything is going on in the child's life that might be affecting her mood or behavior. Being sensitive to your gut feelings is a way of listening to your heart as you try to do what's best for each child.

Giving Yourself Time to Practice Observation

Becoming a skillful observer takes time, practice, and a commitment to the process of regular observation. It is just like anything else in life that you want to do well. When you are learning to ride a bike, you try again and again until you are able to ride with ease. You may not feel very confident at first. But eventually you are on your own, riding down the street thinking, "I can do this! It's not so hard after all." The next step is refining your newfound abilities with a bike. You learn how to use the brakes and the handlebars effectively. Pretty soon you are zooming down the road, the wind blowing in your hair. You are not giving much thought to the individual steps involved in bike riding. You've put the whole process together through practice. It's the same process with learning to do observation well. Every time you try, the process becomes a little easier and more satisfying.

It is important to give yourself the time to practice observation. No one ever became efficient at anything on the first try. You need to honor your own learning style and think about ways to create the time to practice and learn. That might mean just stepping back for a few minutes each day and jotting down what you see a child doing. Or it could mean working out time with your coworkers every day for each of you to practice writing down what you are seeing. It will be exciting and rewarding for you to see your own growth and progress as you take the time to develop your unique style of observation and documentation.

Becoming Open and Ready for Children

An important part of the observation process is to allow yourself to be in the moment with children, to be open and ready to what they have to show you. Most early educators sincerely enjoy children and have chosen this field because of that enjoyment. Sitting on the floor with an infant and playing peekaboo can be fun as the child squeals with delight when you reveal yourself behind your hands. Singing and dancing with toddlers can bring out the child in you. And seeing the lightbulb turn on as a child masters a new concept or skill is truly rewarding. Being an early educator is taxing as well. You are responsible for the safety of the children in your care. You are constantly vigilant regarding the use of materials, the interactions among children, the next activity in the routine, and instructions from family members. As you care for children, you have a busy task list that is constantly running through your head. You are on the lookout as you make multiple decisions throughout each day.

Add observation and writing down those observations to that task list, and you can feel overwhelmed. However, as we have seen, so much can be learned about children through observing them. Accepting the impor-

Diana: *I think part of it is not to be overwhelmed by it all at first. If you just are overwhelmed, like you can't do the whole thing, take bits and pieces of it and start. You don't have to do it all at the beginning.*

tance of observation and documentation and figuring out ways to do it better will enhance the enjoyment you experience with the children.

How do you become open and ready to be in the moment with children? Taming the voice in your head that is running through the list of your duties is one way. Taking a deep breath, sitting with the children, and listening to them lets you see more clearly what they are doing and what's important to them. Letting their energy and personalities flow over you, remembering to smile and laugh with them, and pausing to reflect on what you are seeing are ways to become more aware. Not being so concerned about the next activity but rather focusing on the present one will help you see things more clearly. Recognizing that you cannot see everything in one day and that you can only write down so much helps release the pressure of documentation and accountability, allowing you to watch and enjoy.

Being open and ready involves remembering to observe children in order to see what they *can* do rather than what they *cannot.* Red flags may still go up in your mind as you see a child struggle with a particular task. However, observing and documenting exactly what the child does will help you reach an informed decision, supported by the evidence of your observation notes, about what the child's strengths are and where extra support and intervention may be needed. For example, five-year-old Grant was born a typically developing child, but a slowly progressing neurological disease caused him to lose his hearing and his mobility. He could crawl along the floor pulling his body with his arms. Grant's teacher, Cami, did not observe Grant for the purpose of identifying everything he could *not* do. Instead, she carefully documented what he did do, what he was capable of. She and her colleagues focused on Grant's crawling abilities and set up obstacle courses of soft cushions in the classroom for Grant to maneuver around. They placed him on the slide in the gym and carefully supported him as he crawled to the sliding board and slid down. They made sure that he could participate in activities in ways the other five-year-olds did by placing him in a standing device that supported his limbs and back. One of his favorite activities was to stand at the sensory table. The smile on Grant's face was contagious! His caregivers were recognizing and supporting his capabilities and were open and ready for him to show them just what he could do.

Thinking of Observation as Research

When observing children, you are collecting information about them just as a scientific researcher does about her topic. You can add to that research by interacting with the children to learn more about their thinking and understanding. Asking open-ended questions or making open-ended comments when conversing with older toddlers and pre-school-age children helps to reveal their thinking and provides a window onto their internal worlds.

Open-ended questions or comments do not have one right answer. Instead, the question invites responses that can go in a variety of directions. For example, "What do you know about that?" "Why do you think so?" and "What happened next?" are open-ended questions. In contrast, closed questions have one correct response. Questions such as "What color is this?" "How many do you have?" and "Where does this puzzle piece go?" are closed questions. Closed questions do not give the questioner any insight into the child's way of thinking or feeling at that particular time. Some children, if they do not know the answer, shut down completely and refuse to answer any more questions.

Here are some open-ended questions and comments taken from *The Creative Curriculum for Preschool* (Dodge, Colker, and Heroman 2002, 177). Notice how children could reply in a multitude of ways depending on the situation, their thinking, and their personalities.

- "I see you are mixing yellow and blue paint. I wonder what new color you will create."
- "Adding water to the sand really changed what you could do with the sand. What did you want to happen when you added the water?"
- "What made you decide to feed the guinea pig now instead of at the end of the day?"
- "You've spent a long time on this building. Tell me about it."

Questions and comments like these elicit more revealing information from children. When you observe a child, it is perfectly appropriate to ask open-ended questions and include them and the child's responses as part of the documentation notes. Here are some examples of anecdotes that include the teacher's questioning. Read them and decide if you have more insight into the child's thinking and problem solving because of the questions the teacher asked.

> **Louisa (5 yrs. 0 mos.)**
After I read a book to the class about sadness and laughter, I ask the children, "What did that book make you think about? How did it make you feel?" Louisa raises her hand and says, "When you're feeling sad, don't feel bad, because it's inside you."

> **Kazyan (4 yrs. 8 mos.)**
Kazyan goes into the science area and takes out eyedroppers and three cups. He sits down at the table and sticks the eyedropper into the water and takes it out. There is no water in the eyedropper. He sticks it back into the water and once again, no water. "Miss Nita, how does this work?" he asks. I ask, "Well, what could you do to make it work?" He says, "I need to get the water in here." I say, "That's right, Kazy. How can you do that?" "I don't know how to get it in there. You need to show me." I take the dropper and say, "Look at the dropper, Kazy. What do you see?" Kazyan says, "I see this black thing and the thing where the water needs to go." "That's right." I then ask him, "How does that black thing feel?" Kazyan says, "It's squishy." "So what do you think you should do with the squishy black thing?" Kazyan takes the dropper, holds it on the black, squishy end, and presses his fingers together. "I need to squeeze it together." He places the eyedropper in the water, squeezes, and after a few tries fills the dropper with water again and again. With a big smile he announces, "I did it!"

Sometimes offering open-ended questions or comments helps children to solve disagreements on their own. Here are two examples in which the teacher's comments did that.

> **Yasmina (4 yrs. 2 mos.)**
Yasmina is sitting in the quiet area when Jacob comes and sits beside her. He takes a book away from her. Yasmina says, "Hey, I was looking at that first!" Jacob says, "Me too!" Yasmina says, "Teacher, Jacob is taking the book." I say, "Do you think he wants to look with you?" Yasmina nods her head yes. She tells Jacob, "Okay. Jacob, sit by me and we can read it together." She places part of it on her lap and the other half on Jacob's. She says, "See, I can share."

> **Max (5 yrs. 7 mos.)**
Max and his buddies are riding the scooters on the bike path. They leave and go to play with the wagon and mud. Max returns five minutes later, and Claudia is on the scooter he has been using. Max grabs the handles of the scooter and says, "Hey, I was using that. That's my scooter." Claudia does not get off the scooter and says, "Well, you left and were doing something else." Max holds on tight and repeats, "It's my turn. I was using it." This standoff continues until Max calls my name and says, "Tracy, I was using this scooter." I approach them and say, "It looks like you both want the

same scooter. I wonder what you could do so both of you are happy." Max replies, "We could take turns, and I'm first." "How many times would you like to go around?" I ask. "Five," says Max. "Two," says Claudia. "Five," says Max. "Three," says Claudia. "Five," says Max. "Six," says Claudia. "Five," says Max. "Okay, five," says Claudia. Claudia gets off and lets Max get on the scooter. After five times around, he gives the scooter to her.

Sometimes, reflecting back to the child in an open and ready manner provides her with an opportunity to surprise you with her thinking and problem solving, as in this example.

> **Ayiana (5 yrs. 2 mos.)**
> *Today in circle time all the children are gathering around a song poster on the wall to take turns identifying the letters of the alphabet. Everyone is sitting on his or her knees. They are in three rows. Some of the kids can't see the song on the wall because the person in front of them is taller than they are. Ayiana says, "I know what to do." I ask her, "What would you do?" She gets up and begins moving the taller kids to the back row. Then Ayiana has the rest of the kids stand up so she can see "who is the short-est." She picks out the "short" kids and puts them in front. "Now everyone can see," Ayiana says with a smile. And they can!*

Giving Yourself Time to Reflect on Your Observations

Teachers need time for reviewing observations to consider each child's accomplishments and needs and to plan effectively for the next steps to support continued growth and development. Making a commitment to reflect on your observations, and giving yourself the gift of time to do so, will help make your observations useful in your work with the children. Looking over your written observations and thinking about them will show you patterns. You may suddenly notice that many children have trouble with a certain transition in your day or a certain area of the room. Or you might see that a given child always does better in the afternoon after nap.

Not all reflection has to occur in a quiet, after-hours setting. You may set aside time to reflect about the children by yourself, or you may engage in a conversation with your colleagues. There are many opportunities for reflection:

- Spontaneously at the time of the observation
- Continually, throughout the day, as you observe the child in other activities and routines and piece together a whole picture

- In daily personal reflection in a planned, quiet time
- In daily or weekly group discussions with colleagues
- In ongoing review (perhaps weekly) as you organize and file your documentation
- In a planned reflection to look over the documentation you have completed after several weeks of observing a child

The most important question to consider when reflecting about your observations is: What have I learned about this child? You can go on to ask more detailed questions:

- What are his interests? What really turns him on?
- What are his personality traits? Just who is he?
- What are his accomplishments, and where has he made progress?
- In what particular areas does he experience challenge or difficulty?
- What have my colleagues and I done with him that has worked well?
- What has not worked well with him?
- What changes should we consider?
- What goals should we set?

Taking the time to consider these questions and making plans accordingly will help you be much more in tune with the children. Your job will be easier because you will read their signals more clearly, anticipating trouble and heading it off, building on the successes that have gone before, and helping each child continue to experience even more success. And sometimes reflection time is the only time you have to record your observations. In Chapter 3 we will discuss using this time for documentation more fully.

Becoming Aware of Your Own Biases

Observing children in action is a human endeavor, not a mechanical one. Therefore, total objectivity is not possible. As an early educator watching children at work or at play, you are influenced by your own life experiences, your understanding of child development, your attitudes about yourself and others, and your inherent biases and prejudices. We all look at the world through various lenses. Lack of experience with cultures other than your own or misunderstandings of others' values can influence the way you may interpret what a child is doing. To be a truly effective observer, you must continually develop your own awareness and identify the lenses through which you are looking so that your documented observations represent the child's actual performance. Such self-scrutiny is an ongoing process that takes maturity, thought, reflection, and openness to new ideas.

The Teaching Tolerance Project (1997, 194–95) makes the following recommendation: "Teachers who strive to support the positive development of children's identities and relationships must first be willing to scrutinize their own self-image and its potential influence on classroom life. . . . Research suggests that self-acceptance [of one's racial or ethnic heritage] is essential for responding positively to the race and ethnicity of others." Sometimes conflicts arise between teachers' cultural backgrounds and those of the families and children with whom they work. Differences in views on issues such as feeding and sleeping, attachment and separation, play, exploration, and socialization can all become sources of miscommunication. Misunderstandings about cultural practices can lead to incorrect assumptions about a child's behavior. No one belief system is right or wrong. Educating yourself by talking with children's families about their traditions and approaches to child-rearing will help broaden your understanding of children's actions. As you develop your own awareness of how your experience with different cultures affects your perceptions, you will grow as an observer and be able to see what children do through a clearer lens.

In the reflection activities at the end of this chapter are several self-awareness activities from the authors of *Anti-Bias Curriculum: Tools for Empowering Young Children* (1989). Going through these activities by yourself or with a trusted friend or group of colleagues will help you think carefully about the lens through which you are observing children. Identifying the possible ways that your lens is incorrect or foggy, not giving a true picture of the child, will make your observations far more reliable and informative. You will come to understand not only who you are but also the wonderful richness and diversity of the children and families you serve.

> **Darlisa:** *As I organized my observation notes, the thing that was really amazing, humbling, and surprising to me was that I saw the children much differently than I did when observing in the classroom. Sitting back, reflecting, and reading really helped me. I felt like the Grinch whose heart started growing.*

Documenting Factually

To do observation well, it is critical that the written observations are factual and descriptive notes rather than interpretive, judgmental ones. Since each person sees a situation or a child through the filters of her own unique experience, writing down observations as objectively and factually as possible helps eliminate inherent bias. Objectivity means seeing and recording what is actually taking place, trying not to be influenced by value judgments or inherent biases, and not recording interpretations of the behaviors being observed. It means separating out the pieces, factually describing what you see, and then going back at a later time and interpreting the facts that have been written down. Easy to say, not so easy to do—especially with children whom you work with often and know well. However, the more you observe children, the better you will write objectively.

Here is a subjective, interpretive anecdote. Notice how judgment and evaluation give it a more negative tone.

> Joshua (4 yrs. 3 mos.)
> Joshua was very bad today at circle time. He never listens or sits still. He always wiggles and disturbs his neighbor, and I have to sit with him and hold him.

Certain words stand out in this description of Joshua at circle time: "bad," "never," "always," "disturbs." The problem with these words is the variety of ways they can be perceived by different people. One adult might define "bad" as hitting another child or kicking a chair, while another might define "bad" as not listening to the teacher or talking out of turn. The words "always" and "never" are not good descriptive words to use. They are too broad for this one incident with Joshua. The word "disturbs" can also have multiple meanings that lead us to question exactly what Joshua did that disturbed his neighbors. Was he leaning against them? Whispering in their ears? Pinching, hitting, or kicking? Asking them questions? And finally in this anecdote the tone of the last phrase, "and I have to sit with him and hold him," reflects a negative attitude on the part of the observer, as if he resents having to intervene in this manner to help Joshua be successful at circle time.

It is easy to see that this observation record is interpretive and judgmental. However, there is a way to describe Joshua's behavior at circle time so that the anecdote is factual and descriptive. This gives anyone who reads it the information that tells exactly what Joshua did and said. Based on that information, then, the reader can make her own judgment and determine what the next steps would be for Joshua. Analyze the following rewritten anecdote about Joshua to see how interpretation is replaced by description.

> Joshua (4 yrs. 3 mos.)
> Joshua jumped up and down from his seat at circle time, sitting still for approximately one minute at a time, and then getting up and standing or walking away. Each time, I brought him back to the circle and sat him back down. When sitting, he poked the child next to him and talked to him. I sat down with Joshua and asked him if he would sit on my lap. He agreed. He leaned against my chest, sucked his thumb, and listened to the story for five minutes.

In this factual description, you can see that Joshua has trouble sitting still and participating in group time until he is placed in an adult's lap. Then he settles down. Therefore, any curriculum planning for him at group times should include the opportunity for him to sit with an adult so that he can successfully participate in the activities with the large group.

Following is a chart from the book *Focused Portfolios: A Complete Assessment for the Young Child* (Gronlund and Engel 2001, 97). Look over the words and phrases in the left-hand column and notice how many of those you see in the first observation about Joshua, as well as in the subjective anecdotes below. Then, when reading the factual and descriptive anecdotes on later pages, refer back to this chart to see how the words and phrases change from evaluative and interpretive to factual and descriptive, as in the right-hand column of the chart.

Words & Phrases to Avoid	Words & Phrases to Use
• The child loves . . .	• He often chooses . . .
• The child likes . . .	• I saw him . . .
• He enjoys . . .	• I heard her say . . .
• She spends a long time at . . .	• He spends five minutes doing . . .
• It seems like . . .	• She said . . .
• It appears . . .	• Almost every day he . . .
• I thought . . .	• Once or twice a month, she . . .
• I felt . . .	• Each time, he . . .
• I wonder . . .	• She consistently . . .
• He does . . . very well . . .	• We observed a pattern of . . .
• She is bad at . . .	
• This is difficult for . . .	

Analyze the rest of these anecdotes for the words and phrases they contain that are not factual and descriptive.

> Jennifer (6 mos.)
> Jennifer is a very fussy baby. She cries when her mom leaves. She demands a lot of adult attention. She has trouble settling down unless she has her pacifier or is being held. She startles easily and gets upset when other toddlers come near her.

> Carrie (3 yrs. 2 mos.)
> Carrie runs outside to the bikes at riding time because she wants to have first choice of the bikes. She always wants the red bike and forgets the rule of walking outside to the bike area.

> Max (2 yrs. 6 mos.)
> During art time today, Max really enjoys painting a picture. He uses up a lot of paint—green, blue, brown, and red. His picture is very interesting. It looks like he painted some people and a house. Max paints almost every day, and it seems to be his favorite activity.

Here is an example of an observation note that is written with no opinion or judgment included, only a description of what the child did and said. Note that quoting a child is a form of factually describing what occurred.

> Lupita (2 yrs. 5 mos.)
> At lunch, Lupita sees Lorrain put chile on her burrito. Lupita says, "Mama chile." Lorrain asks her if her mom eats chiles, and Lupita says, "Sí." When she wants more food, she says, "Más [more]," and when we ask her to say, "Por favor [please]," she promptly complies. Later, she watches Jason eat. She points to him and says, "Mira, Jason!" [Look, Jason!].

The reader of this anecdote has a good sense of how Lupita uses language at lunchtime. The context of the situation is described as well as the teachers' interaction with Lupita. There is no evaluation of Lupita's language skills. Instead, there is reporting of her words and phrases.

Here are two other factual and descriptive anecdotes to consider.

> Naomi (7 mos.)
> Naomi is sitting in the bouncer with the jungle gym hanging over her. She is in the bouncer for a couple of minutes when she starts to cry. Her mom is in the room fixing a bottle for her. Mom says, "I hear you, sweetie. I'll be right there." Naomi places both hands together in a fist and places it over her mouth. She starts to move her fist back and forth and babbles, "Ba, ba, ba, ba." This continues for a few minutes until Mom picks her up and feeds her the bottle.

Johanna: *I found it very freeing to be able to just write what they are doing. I enjoyed that. It freed me from having to evaluate it while I was observing. I could just write what they did.*

Diana: *One of the challenges is being able to write it the right, correct way, where you're not putting your judgments in or you're just barely writing anything down.*

> Garrett (5 yrs. 1 mo.)
>
> Garrett asks me to read The Very Hungry Caterpillar. When it says, "That night he had a stomachache," Garrett says, "Well, he ate all of the food in the world." I read the part where he built a small house, and Garrett says, "It's a cocoon." I reply, "Yes, Garrett, it's a cocoon." After the book is finished, Garrett says, "One time at my grandma's house, I saw a cocoon. But the next night, it did not turn into a butterfly. It stayed a cocoon."

Interpreting Children's Actions

You may be wondering where judgment, evaluation, and interpretation fit into the observation process. The problem with interpretation is that there may be several possible ways to look at a child's actions. You want to be sure that you have enough evidence to support any conclusions you are making about a child. Read the following description of Elijah in the block area.

> Elijah (3 yrs. 9 mos.)
>
> Elijah is in the block area. He has several animals in his hand. Several other children are in this area with him. He runs around in circles with the animals, and another child chases him. He laughs and screams, "You can't catch me."

When reading this anecdote you can draw many different conclusions about Elijah's actions even though you don't know him. You may decide that he is out of control and desperately needs adult intervention to help him settle down. Or you may think that he is running off extra energy. You may determine that he is a threat to other children in the area or that he is only expressing the joy and exuberance of a young child.

The facts on hand from this one observation are not enough to know which conclusion is the correct one. Therefore, if you move too quickly to a judgment about Elijah's behavior, you may very well be mistaken. Instead, the only way to be sure of your interpretation is to observe Elijah many more times in a variety of situations to see how he handles his energy and exuberance. Then the record of his actions will provide a growing collection of evidence about Elijah. From that record you will be able to determine how best to help and support him in the classroom.

The process of writing down your thoughts, ideas, and interpretations needs to be kept separate to ensure objectivity. Some teachers use a format for documentation that includes both the factual description and their interpretation. They divide their paper into two columns, one for writing down the actions of the child, the other for writing the possibilities for interpreting those actions. We have designed a form for you to use to record factual observations and possible interpretations. You can find in it Appendix A. Often they follow those possibilities with a question mark because they recognize that they do not really know exactly why the child is doing what she is doing. This helps them to remember that their interpretations need to be continually readjusted as more situations are observed.

The following chart shows the Elijah observation recorded in this way.

Facts	Possible Interpretations
Elijah is in the block area. He has several animals in his hand. Several other children are in this area with him. He runs around in circles with the animals, and another child chases him. He laughs and screams, "You can't catch me."	• Is he out of control and desperately needing adult intervention to help him settle down? • Is he running off extra energy that day? Is he that energetic every day? • Is he a threat to other children in the area? • Is he merely expressing his joy and exuberance?

The next step in this process is using the information, both fact and interpretation, to plan intervention strategies that will ensure success for the child and maximize his potential to develop and learn. As multiple observations are recorded factually and descriptively, you can review them, thinking about the evidence they present. For Elijah, multiple observations may show a pattern emerging that he is a very expressive child, showing his joy in just being alive. Then his providers might choose to sit back and laugh with him, give him hugs, and join him in his positive approach to his days at preschool. On the other hand, multiple observations may show that he is often out of control. In that case, his teachers will provide him with adult guidance and protect other children. Steps would be planned to help him throughout every day so that he works toward developing self-control through using words to express his feelings, pounding a pillow when angry, going to a teacher for help, and so on. In Chapter 5 we will explore in-depth curricular planning based on observational documentation.

Not Missing Any Children

To do observation well, you must make a commitment to attempt to observe each child. This does not mean that you write down everything you see children doing. Instead, you identify the important things in specific areas of development that give a well-rounded and complete picture of who each child is, what she is capable of, what he is working on, and what you are doing to help her be successful. As you attempt to run a busy classroom and to provide loving care for a group of children, you may find yourself paying attention to some children more than others. Some children demand your attention. They may act out or need help with their own self-control. Having an adult nearby who helps them to learn to express their feelings appropriately and not hurt other children is essential. Other children demand attention by looking to you for love and affection, for praise and validation. These are the children who continually bring drawings or paintings to you, who say things like, "Look what I did, Teacher!" or "I love you." They are asking for positive attention. The observational records of children who demand negative or positive attention are often filled with notes. Teachers generally report that they do not have difficulty remembering to document these children's accomplishments.

> **Robin:** *A lot of times, it's very easy to focus and do observations on those children who are very active and who are leading through the room. And sometimes it's the children who are quieter and keep to themselves— sometimes it's a challenge for me, at least, to try to zone in on them and try to capture and celebrate all of their milestones as well.*

There is also often a group of children who can be identified as "invisible" when it comes to their observation records. These are the children who do not ask for a lot of attention. In fact, these are often children who are comfortable going about their days in the early childhood classroom quite independently and successfully. Because these children are not requiring an adult's intervention very often, teachers report that this is the group about whom they tend to have less documentation. They're easier to miss. It's easy to say, "Oh, I'll remember that later," and then forget to write it down. When observation is the source of information for assessment purposes, for accountability purposes, for reflection and planning purposes, no child can be missed.

Observation Practice: Factual versus Interpretive Anecdotes

Purpose: To learn to write what is actually seen and record what is taking place rather than write anecdotes that are influenced by value judgments and interpretation

What to Do: If you have access to the *Focused Observations* video, watch Vignette 2, "Blocks," which shows Alex (5 yrs. 2 mos.) and Matthew (4 yrs. 10 mos.). Before watching the vignette, decide which boy to focus on (Alex is in the Batman shirt; Matthew is in the Spiderman shirt), and write down everything you see that child doing. If you do not have the *Focused Observations* video, watch a child during a play time, and write down everything you see the child doing.

Group Discussion: If you're watching the video as a group, create a list of things that the group observed. Discuss the difference between factual and interpretive anecdotes. Decide as a group which comments are factual and which are interpretive. If observing a child in your classroom, review your documentation, and note your own use of factual words and interpretive words. Were you surprised by what you discovered about your use of words? Be prepared to discuss your own thinking about factual and interpretive words and phrases with others.

Observation Practice: Using the Facts/Interpretation Form

Purpose: To learn another way to distinguish between fact and interpretation when writing anecdotes

What to Do: If you have access to the *Focused Observations* video, watch Vignette 3, "Dramatic Play," which shows Paris (5 yrs. 5 mos.), Kelsey (3 yrs. 10 mos.), and Keyonna (3 yrs. 5 mos.). If you do not have the *Focused Observations* video, watch two or more children playing together. You may focus on one of the children or attempt to document what you see each of them doing. Use the Facts/Interpretation Form found in Appendix A to record your observation, editing as you watch the children to separate your factual description of what they are doing from your interpretation of their actions.

Group Discussion: Share your observations with the group, and discuss how you separated the facts from your interpretations. Did the use of the form help you in this process? Why or why not?

Reflection

What to Do: Consider the following questions:

- What steps will you take to give yourself time to practice observing and documenting?
- In what ways are you open and ready to observe what children can do?
- Identify a time when your own opinions or biases influenced your thinking about a child.

Finding Your Observation Style

Purpose: To identify the characteristics of your personal observation style and help you strategize to make your observations more objective

What to Do: Review the chart "Words and Phrases to Avoid/Words and Phrases to Use" on page 29. Identify some of the phrases you tend to use, and write them in your journal.

Think of ways you can move toward more objective documentation. What steps will you take to work on this part of documentation? Write a list of steps in your journal.

Write out your answers and thoughts for the following self-awareness activities (Derman-Sparks et al. 1989, 112):

- How would you describe your racial/ethnic identity, your gender identity, your differences in physical abilities? What is important and not important to you about these aspects of yourself? How do you feel about these identities?
- How did you learn about your racial/ethnic identity? Your gender identity? Your physical abilities and limitations? What are your earliest memories? What was fun or painful as you learned about these aspects of your identity?
- In what ways do you agree or disagree with your parents' views about race, ethnicity, gender, and physical abilities? If you disagree, how did you develop your own ideas? Who were significant influences on you? What do you plan to teach your own children?

References

- Derman-Sparks, Louise, and the A.B.C. Task Force. 1989. *Anti-bias curriculum: Tools for empowering young children.* Washington, D.C.: National Association for the Education of Young Children.

- Dodge, Diane Trister, Laura J. Colker, and Cate Heroman. 2002. *The creative curriculum for preschool.* 4th edition. Washington, D.C.: Teaching Strategies.

- Gronlund, Gaye, and Bev Engel. 2001. *Focused portfolios: A complete assessment for the young child.* St. Paul: Redleaf.

- The Teaching Tolerance Project. 1997. *Starting small: Teaching tolerance in preschool and the early grades.* Montgomery, Ala.: Southern Poverty Law Center.

chapter 3

Preschool Choi

Date _Feb. 10_

(may be used to tally one child's choice

Child(ren)

Art	
11 mins	Social/Emotic

nipulatives	
mirs.	
0	

How Do You Fit In Observation?

You may be wondering how you are going to manage to observe children, write down your observations, and still interact fully with the children. You do so by figuring out the best times to observe and by trying different recording methods. There is no one right time or perfect method. You may find some methods are a better fit than others for your way of teaching or your own organizational style. Taking the time to experiment, talking with colleagues, and then reflecting on what feels most comfortable to you are important steps to help you be successful.

When to Observe and Write

You will discover what works best for you as you experiment with different times to fit in documentation. We recommend that you try writing observation notes at the following times:

- In the moment with the child
- As soon as possible after the event
- Stepping out of the action in teamwork with your colleagues
- In reflection

In the Moment with the Child

You have most likely experienced the thrill of seeing a child accomplish something and wanting to remember and document the activity. What you observed might fit into developmental criteria. It might be reflective of the child's achieving a certain milestone. You might be seeing the child do something for the first time. You recognize that what you are seeing is important and should be written down as quickly as possible. So you grab your clipboard or notepad, and you record your observation right then.

The advantage of being able to observe and document what you are seeing right away is that you are capturing the authentic, spontaneous actions of children. Because you are recording so close to the event, it is easier for you to remember details and direct quotes of the child's language. In order to do this you must be prepared by having writing tools handy. Teachers have written down these moments on scraps of paper with crayons or anything that was close by and could be used. The notes written in the moment may be brief, highlighting the basics of what the child did. You may want to fill in the missing details at a later time.

As Soon as Possible After the Event

Another time for documentation is as soon as possible after the event. Sometimes you are just too busy with the children and cannot write down an observation as it is occurring. You might be busy cleaning up after snack when you observe a child across the room doing something that you want to document. Your job is to finish cleaning up rather than worry about finding writing materials. So you observe the child while you wash up, trying hard to focus on the details you want to remember, and then document what you have seen as soon as possible after the fact. The advantage of this type of documentation is that you are able to observe and still complete the tasks of running a classroom.

But there are also some disadvantages to waiting to document until after the event.

- *You may forget important details.* The longer you wait to document something, the more likely you are to forget parts of the activity or behavior that was observed. The sooner you are able to write it down, the more likely you are to remember it accurately.

- *It's hard to document complete language samples awhile after you heard them.* Remembering after the fact every word that a child has said is close to impossible. The best you can do is to get the gist of what he said, hopefully with a few direct quotes included.

> **Pam:** *I used the back of a paper bag in the room to write observations on because I couldn't find any paper. But they had this great conversation going, and I was actually going to be able to write everything down. I found a paper bag and a pencil, and I'm writing on the back of a paper bag!*

■ *It's harder to remain objective and descriptive in the anecdote.*
   The more time that passes between the initial actions of the child
   and the documentation of those actions, the more you may tend
   to write down interpretations of what happened instead of simply
   a factual description. Internally editing yourself as you write
   down observations after the event will help you keep the anecdote objective.

Stepping Out of the Action

For those of you teaching in teams, another way to observe and document is to step out of the daily action for a while. This is a wonderful way
to learn about children because your only responsibilities are listening,
watching, and writing. You and your colleagues must decide who will
step out of the action; when that will fit into the day; and who will super-
vise the children. This takes coordination, communication, and planning.
For example, during a story-reading time with the large group, one
teacher may read the story and attempt to maintain the interest and
engagement of all the children. The other teacher may then sit near the
story area and take notes during the reading activity. She is always ready
to step back into the action if something happens—if a child's safety is
of concern or if her colleague needs help with a child's behavior. Then
the observation and documentation stop, and she interacts with the children as needed.

Stepping out of the action may also happen spontaneously. There
will be occasional moments when the children are all busily engaged.
You look around the room and realize that none of the children needs
your intervention or assistance. This is the time to take a few minutes to
sit with your clipboard and write what you are seeing them do. You might
observe a specific child you have been wondering about or a group of
children involved in an activity. Again, you are always ready to step back
into the action if the children need you. Realistically, the older the children in the class, the more likely this may occur. For infants and toddlers,
stepping out of the action may happen infrequently. Infant and toddler
teachers almost always need to be available to the young ones in their
care. The growing independence of preschoolers may allow for more
times when watching children in this manner is possible.

The advantage of observing and documenting out of the action is that
you are able to concentrate more fully on what you are observing and
documenting. You may be able to write a very detailed description at this
time or include language samples with direct quotes from a child. Many

different recording methods can be effective because you can look across the classroom for a longer period of time, following one specific child's choices and time engagements or tracking several children at a time. The disadvantage is the planning and coordination with colleagues involved and the interruptions that can occur when you need to step back in and assist the children.

In Reflection

Reflection is an important part of the process of observation and documentation. Sitting down at naptime or at the end of the day and reflecting back on what you have seen are sometimes the only realistic ways to document what has happened with the children in your care. This is especially true for those of you who spend your days as the only adult with a group of children. In order to use reflection time most effectively, you can help jog your memory with a variety of cues: photographs, brief notes, conversations with colleagues, and work samples.

During your time with the children, you might only have time to document their actions with photographs but not to sit and write down what you have observed. Or you might have jotted down very brief notes or used a check sheet to help remind you of what you want to remember about the children that day. Then you can use those photos and brief notes at naptime, the end of the day, or even at the end of the week to help you remember what went on. If you use a digital camera, you can look over the photos at the end of the day. If you have to have film developed, you may have to wait some time before retrieving the images. If this is the case, keeping a list of the photos taken, with brief notes next to each photo number, will help fill in the details you want to remember. Saving children's drawings, paintings, writing samples, or other creations may also help you to remember the details of the observation.

When you spend time reflecting at the end of the day or week, those of you working in teaching teams will find that talking with your colleagues helps everyone's memory. Assigning the writing tasks among the group helps to divide up the workload of documentation. Taking a few minutes at home is another way to use reflection as a means of recalling the activities in the course of the day. Early childhood professionals often find that they think about the children in their care even after leaving the workday. Taking a moment to write down those thoughts helps to add to the collection of observation information you are putting together for each child.

The advantage of documenting in reflection is that it fits into the context of a busy and active day with children. Reflective anecdotes tend to be more of a summary in nature. And this can be an advantage: when looking back, you have the whole picture in mind. You can think through the events of the day and place the child's actions in context. The written observation can cover several times of the day and note any patterns in the child's behavior and interactions. Noting how the child has gone about a task in the past as compared to that day helps to document the progress the child is making.

The downside is that it is difficult to remember an event after a long day. And if you wait until the end of the week, recalling exactly what happened is very hard. Details become cloudy, and objectivity is always a concern. The more you can use various cues to jog your memory, the more successful this type of documentation will be.

> **Pam:** *I had a small class and no assistant this year. What I found that worked well for me was taking more photographs. I had a running list and would jot down brief notes about the photos. And then when I got my pictures in, I could put them together.*

Where to Write Observations

There are many different materials and some time-saving formats and technologies to use when writing down your observations. In this section we explore the following possibilities to help you realistically and practically fit observation in with your supervision of the children.

- Easily transportable ways of recording: sticky notes, index cards, binders, and clipboards
- Ways to see all of the children's names at one time so no one is missed: blank address-size labels, Quick Check Recording Sheets, Brief Notes Recording Sheets, and file folders with sticky notes or index cards
- Recording devices: audio, video, handheld dictating machines, and other handheld electronic devices

Sometimes it's most important to have something in your pocket or available nearby to grab quickly in order to write down what you are seeing. Sticky-note pads, index cards, notebooks, and clipboards can all be easily transported around the classroom and used to write down anecdotal information. Some teachers carry sticky pads (generally 3 by 5 inch or larger) and a pen in their pockets or work aprons at all times in order to jot notes down quickly. Such pads are now available with lined paper in a 5 by 7 inch size to allow for more room to include child quotes and detailed observation notes. Other providers use small spiral-bound notebooks of index cards. The cards are perforated for easy removal to place in a child's file at a later time. These kinds of notebooks are also small enough to carry (with a pen) around the classroom. Small spiral-bound notebooks with lined paper can also be used. Some observers prefer a three-ring binder with lined or unlined paper. Many divide the binder into sections for each child. They may also prepare the papers for each child ahead of time so that specific areas for observation are identified. See the example of an Observation Record that follows. A form ready to copy and use can be found in Appendix A.

Three-ring binders are larger and must be carried around the classroom in order to be handy for quick documentation. One solution is to have more than one binder with the same setup. They can be placed in various spots throughout the room and are easily available when needed. Clipboards are also easily transported around the room. Some teachers use clipboards with notebook paper to write down general comments.

In order to be more focused on specific children, some teachers place sheets of blank address-size labels on a clipboard and print the children's names on them. This helps to make sure that no child is missed. Instead of labels, clipboards can also hold a piece of paper with a class list or a Quick Check Recording Sheet with all of the children's names on it. See Appendix A for a form ready to copy and use.

This format for recording is quick and easy to use, especially when working with a small group of children. You can jot down information about more than one child at a time and still be interacting with them, guiding the activity at hand.

For some observations, making check marks or very brief notes is appropriate. For others, this format will not work. The Quick Check

---

Observation Record

Child's Name _____

Language	Social/Emotional

Physical (gross and fine motor)	Creative

Cognitive (math, problem-solving)	Early Literacy (reading & writing)

©2005 Gaye Gronlund and Marlyn James. May be reproduced for use by teachers.

Recording Sheet can be used when a yes or no question is being asked. Look at the first column of the completed Quick Check Recording Sheet below. The question asked is "Does this child cut with scissors easily?" For those children for whom the answer was yes, the teacher made a check mark. For those children for whom the answer was no, she left the space blank. You can decide what kind of mark you want to make (such as an "X" or a "no") to help keep the information clear for future reference.

The second column of the completed sheet below shows another way to record brief notes in this format. The question was "Does this child count to five with one-to-one correspondence?" In this case the answers were recorded with a check mark for those who did count to five with one-to-one correspondence and, for those who did differently, with the number to which each child counted with one-to-one correspondence (for one child it was only three, while for another it was twenty).

Sometimes you may want to include more information but still want to keep your notes very short. The Brief Notes Recording Sheet that follows can help keep the full list of children you are observing in front of you and let you write down more than just a check mark or a yes or no. See Appendix A for a form ready to copy and use.

Quick Check Recording Sheet

Children's Names	Date & Activity	Date & Activity	Date & Activity	Date & Activity

©2005 Gaye Gronlund and Marlyn James. May be reproduced for use by teachers.

Quick Check Recording Sheet

Children's Names	Date & Activity cuts w/ scissors easily 9/14	Date & Activity counts to 5 w H 9/20	Date & Activity	Date & Activity
Ashley	✓	✓		
Brian		✓ 3		
Cameron				
David	✓	✓ 20		
Ebony		✓		

Brief Notes Recording Sheet

Children's Names	Date & Activity

©2005 Gaye Gronlund and Marlyn James. May be reproduced for use by teachers.

This form might be used when you are sitting with children helping them listen to your colleague read a story. You might note next to each child's name who was responding to the story by asking questions or making related comments. Or if you are working with a small group of children on creating patterns with colored beads, you would have more room to write down the information about each child's pattern.

By using blank address-size labels, a class list, or a recording sheet on a clipboard, you see exactly who has been observed and who has been missed. This helps make sure that no child is neglected when it comes to observations. Again, clipboards must be carried around the classroom in order to be handy for quick documentation. As with three-ring binders, one solution is to have more than one clipboard with the same setup so that they can be placed in various spots throughout the room and are easily available when needed.

File folders are also easily transported around the classroom. You can use a file folder that contains sticky notes or index cards on which to write. Here are two easy-to-make designs for file folder documentation:

A File Folder with Sticky Notes

1. Open a file folder, and lay it flat.
2. Using a ruler and marker, divide the folder into boxes, one for each child. (A letter-size file folder can be divided into twenty-four approximately 3 by 3 inch boxes. If you are responsible for fewer than twenty-four children or want more space and larger notes, make the boxes larger.)

3. Label the boxes with each of the children's names.
4. Place sticky notes into these boxes as observations are written on them.

Folder with Index Cards

1. Open a file folder, and lay it flat.
2. Using clear tape, layer the index cards from bottom to top so that only the bottom inch or so of the card is visible. Up to fifteen index cards can fit on each side of the file folder.
3. On that bottom inch of each card, write a child's name.
4. Write observations for each child on the cards, flipping up the other cards as necessary. When a card is full, it can easily be removed and replaced with another.

Technological advances are providing new tools to use in recording observations. Video and audio taping are two familiar possibilities for recording young children's actions and emerging language. They provide immediate recording capabilities and can help to document a lot of information at one time. The problem with these methods is that you must review the video or audio tape and determine what portions are significant and how best to use them. So a reflection and review time, plus plans for writing down the information recorded, must be included when using these technologies.

PDAs (personal digital assistants) can be used to record brief observations such as key words to remember for a later time. Handheld tape recorders or dictating machines can record your descriptions of what children are doing and saying. These devices also require a reflection and review time to write down what was learned.

> **Robin:** *One of the biggest time-savers is a tape recorder. We strategically place it so that the children don't find it. We use a voice-activated tape recorder so that we can catch the conversations that are going on. We might put it over in the block area so we can hear different things that they say. Later, we listen to it and write their language down.*

How Much to Write

How much to write depends on the purpose for the documentation as well as the format that best fits that purpose. The recording sheets will not work when you are trying to capture children's use of language or describing how they went about solving a problem with materials or resolving a disagreement with another child. In these circumstances you will need to write more of a description. The situation may determine the length of the written description. If you have time, as well as the luxury of being undisturbed, you may be able to record everything the child says and does. If you are busily engaged with other children, your memory may not catch every detail. You may have to summarize the child's actions in your description. Your personal style of writing can also influence how much you write. Some prefer to write in complete sentences and tell a story. Others tend to be list makers who highlight the important things they saw the child do in bulleted points on the page.

In this section we talk about three formats for observation:

- running records
- summative anecdotes
- lists

Running Records

To do a running record well, you step out of the action and remain undisturbed so that you can capture on paper everything you are seeing the child do and hearing her say. So you will need to coordinate with your colleagues to make sure that the children are well supervised while you observe. A clipboard and notepaper are more helpful for this type of documentation because you will write more than with some of the other formats. This type of observation requires writing fast! You may need to develop a shorthand or series of abbreviations for yourself. Many teachers will identify children by the first letter of their first name. A running record also requires intense focus. Setting a time limit and staying true to it helps to make this task more manageable. Five minutes may be about the maximum amount of time to allot so that you are not exhausted trying to watch and write for a longer period. This form of documentation is helpful but not always easily implemented because of the need for few distractions. Therefore we do not recommend you use it very often.

Here are two examples of running records.

> Priscylla (2 yrs. 4 mos.)
> Over a two-minute period, Priscylla is sitting on the floor with the shape sorter. Priscylla picks up the square shape with her right hand and pushes it into the square opening. Priscylla picks up the circle shape with her right hand and pushes it into the container. She picks up the triangle shape and pushes it into the triangle-shaped hole.

> Skye (4 yrs. 4 mos.)
> Skye goes to the art area. Over a fifteen-minute period, she gets a brown piece of construction paper. She folds it with both hands. Then with her right hand she cuts blue papers in small rectangle shapes. She puts the

shapes in the folded brown paper. She brings them to me and says, "Here's a book with blue Bandaids." She goes back and folds a light purple paper. She reopens it and closes it several times. She makes a cut on one side and says, "That airplane doesn't work." She gets a dark purple paper, folds it, and makes several cuts in it with the scissors. She brings me both papers and says, "This airplane doesn't work, and here's another kind of airplane." She goes back to the table, cuts some newspaper, and says, "Bigger Bandaids." She gets four pieces of paper and cuts out a shape that she drew. She cuts all four pieces. She comes to me and says, "Here's some bigger Bandaids, and I cut this out." She puts them on the table with the book and airplanes. She goes back, gets another purple paper, a pencil, crayon, glue, rice, and buttons. She turns the glue upside down and then back right side up. Using both hands she squeezes the bottle and turns the lid. She pounds the bottle on the table. She looks at the bottle, pokes the tip with her finger. She twists the top again, then squeezes the glue onto the newspaper that is on the table. Then she glues rice and buttons on the purple paper and draws her "heart helicopter." After she tells me about her picture, she says, "I'm done. Now I'll clean up."

Summative Anecdotes

Running records tend to be long, especially if they take place across a fairly extended period of time, as with the anecdote about Skye. A less time-consuming way to write about a child's extensive involvement is to summarize what she does and says. The summative anecdote is still factual and descriptive in nature, but it does not include every single detail of the child's actions and words. Instead, it gives the highlights.

The last observation note about Skye is very long and detailed. Here are four sentences that summarize Skye's actions and words. Read through them, and see if you still get the same information and understanding of Skye and her capabilities.

> Skye (4 yrs. 4 mos.)
> *Skye goes to the art area and stays for over fifteen minutes folding and cutting papers, using her right hand to cut. She puts the shapes in the folded paper and tells me, "Here's a book with blue Bandaids." She glues rice and buttons on a paper, squeezing and pounding to get the glue out. She tells me her picture is a "heart helicopter," then says, "I'm done. Now I'll clean up."*

This summative anecdote is much shorter. Unimportant details such as the colors of the paper, the exact steps she took to fold and cut each set of papers, and the sequence she followed to unclog the glue bottle are deleted. Those deletions are a judgment call on the part of the writer. If you were Skye's teacher, and you thought her patience and multiple attempts with the glue bottle were an important indicator of how she goes about solving a problem without exhibiting frustration, you might choose to include that information.

Summative anecdotes do involve some judgment in what is included and what is not. However, they provide a more efficient way of recording what children are doing and can be focused to help provide information about specific areas of development. The following summative anecdote gives information about how Adam routinely comforts himself. This note is a compilation of several observations across time. Evaluation and interpretation are still not included; only factual description is written. Yet the reader has a clear picture of how Adam handles himself when upset or sad.

> Adam (1 yr.)
When Adam is getting upset or sad, I have noticed that he comforts himself by sucking on his finger. Adam will also drink his bottle when he is upset. He routinely comforts himself both ways.

As you can see, summative anecdotes are helpful for looking at a child's actions across time.

Lists

Some observers find that writing lists or bulleted points fits their own personal style of thinking more closely than writing out full sentences or telling more of a story in the anecdote. As long as a reader can look at the list and figure out exactly what the child was doing, this type of anecdote can be another effective way to get information down quickly. Here are some examples.

> David (1 yr. 10 mos.)
Today David said, "Lala," "Yello" (Angelo), "airpane," "Dan," "Tash" (trash), "Bu" (blue), and "marka" (marker).

> Jessica (4 yrs. 5 mos.)
At the bathroom, waits her turn to use toilet, talking with other children.
Toilets independently.
Washes her hands with no reminding, using soap.
Laughs and hugs teacher.
Goes to snack table.

As you can see, a list can be especially good for recording a child's spoken words or tracking a sequence of activities in which the child engages.

In order to effectively document what you see children doing, you will need to try out several different formats, thinking about the purpose of your observation, the amount of time you have, and the interruptions you might experience. You will also need to think about your own personal writing style. Finding the right format will help reduce the stress of combining observation and documentation. But it takes time to figure it out. The perfect format for you might be completely different from that of your colleague in the room next door. Part of being successful at this process is to experiment and learn what works best for you.

How Much Detail to Include in Your Observation Notes

Quality documentation can be brief. Good anecdotes are ones that include enough facts so that when another adult reads them, she can clearly picture the child's actions. Here's an example of an anecdote that is missing some key details.

> Tanya (3 yrs. 6 mos.)
> Tanya did a very good job putting together several puzzles in a row.

In analyzing this observation note, you can see that interpretive language was included in saying "a very good job." Instead of writing such a broad, evaluative statement, it would be better to include specific details to help the reader see what is meant by "a very good job." Such details might include the following:

- The type and difficulty of the puzzles. Were these puzzles with knobs, with clear outlines of where the pieces went, or with no clear delineation of where each piece should go? Was there a picture on a box for her to follow, and did she do so?
- The number of pieces in the puzzles
- The number of puzzles she completed
- How Tanya worked: by herself, with another child, or with an adult helping her

Here's a rewritten version of the anecdote about Tanya. This note is longer than the first, but not excessively so. Now the reader has a much clearer idea of how Tanya went about working with puzzles.

> Tanya (3 yrs. 6 mos.)
Tanya goes to the puzzle table and puts together three eight- to ten-piece puzzles with the pieces outlined on the puzzle board. She then takes out a twenty-five-piece floor puzzle and spends ten minutes putting it together, looking back at the picture on the box to check where pieces went. "I did it!" she announces when finished.

It is not necessary to write very lengthy observation notes, as long as the important details are included. Length does not equal quality. Keeping that in mind helps you be more efficient in your use of language as you write about what you have seen the children do.

There are many ways to fit in observation and still have time to interact fully with the children. Planning and flexibility are the keys to success. The process will be more doable when you try out different times to document, experiment with different recording formats, and figure out what works best for you.

Observation Practice: Running Record

Purpose: To practice writing down everything you can that a child does or says in a set period of time

What to Do: If you have access to the *Focused Observations* video, watch Vignette 4, "Making Music," which shows Christian (2 yrs. 7 mos.). Pay close attention, and try to write down all the things Christian does. If you do not have the *Focused Observations* video, watch a child you know during a play time, but limit your time for observing to no more than two minutes.

Remember to be factual and descriptive, not interpretive. Be prepared to share your experience with others.

Group Discussion: Share some of the running records recorded by the group. Discuss the ease or difficulty of trying this type of documentation. Could it be done while you were in the middle of running a busy classroom? How practical is such a recording method for your setting?

Observation Practice: Summative Anecdote

Purpose: To practice writing an observation note that summarizes what you have seen a child do in just two to four sentences

What to Do: If you have access to the *Focused Observations* video, watch Vignette 5, "Painting," which shows Megan (4 yrs. 8 mos.). If you do not have the *Focused Observations* video, watch a child you know during a play time for four to six minutes. Pay close attention to what Megan or the child you know does.

Do not write down your observation while you are watching. Instead, after the vignette or the observation time is over, write down two to four sentences summarizing what you saw Megan or the child in your program do. Remember to be factual and descriptive, not interpretive. Be prepared to share your experience with others.

Group Discussion: Share some of the summative anecdotes recorded by the group. Discuss the ease or difficulty of trying this type of documentation. Could it be done while you were in the middle of running a busy classroom? How practical is such a recording method for your setting?

Observation Practice: Making a List

Purpose: To practice writing an observation note that is a list of what you have seen the child do

What to Do: If you have access to the *Focused Observations* video, watch Vignette 6, "A Toddler in Action," which shows Hunter (1 yr. 10 mos.). If you do not have the *Focused Observations* video, watch a child you know during play. The time of your observation is not as important for this activity; we recommend anywhere from three to five minutes. Pay close attention to the things that Hunter or the other child does. Either as you watch or afterward, make a list of the things you saw the child do. Do not worry about complete sentences or descriptive phrases. Try to be efficient in your use of words. Still remember to be factual and descriptive, not interpretive. Be prepared to share your experience with others.

Group Discussion: Share some of the lists recorded by the group. Discuss the ease or difficulty of trying this type of documentation. Could it be done while you were in the middle of running a busy classroom? How practical is such a recording method for your setting?

Observation Practice: Using the Quick Check Recording Sheet

Purpose: To practice observation and recording by identifying one skill ahead of time and noting the child's accomplishment of that skill quickly on a check sheet

What to Do: If you have access to the *Focused Observations* video, watch Vignette 7, "Three Young Writers," which shows Tyler (4 yrs. 4 mos.), Malik (4 yrs. 5 mos.), and Dontasia (4 yrs. 1 mo.). List their names on a Quick Check Recording Sheet (see Appendix A). These three children will all be using a writing tool to write or draw. Watch the vignette and note with a check mark which of the children write their names approximately.

If you do not have the *Focused Observations* video, watch a small group of children matching colors, writing, or drawing. List the children's names on a Quick Check Recording Sheet (see Appendix A). For the children who are matching colors, make a check mark next to the names of the ones who are able to match colors accurately. For children who are writing or drawing, watch and note with a check mark which children hold the writing tools correctly in their hands (rather than with a fist or other kind of grasp). Be prepared to share your experience with others.

Group Discussion: Share some of the check sheets recorded by the group. Discuss the ease or difficulty of trying this type of documentation. Could it be done while you were in the middle of running a busy classroom? How practical is such a recording method for your setting?

Observation Practice: Documenting Observation of a Group of Children

Purpose: To practice writing observation information about a group of children

What to Do: If you have access to the *Focused Observations* video, watch Vignette 8, "Pancakes Story," which shows a group of three- to five-year-old children. If you do not have the *Focused Observations* video, watch a group of children listening to a story. Your observation should take place over at least five minutes. Before watching this vignette or observing children, determine what specific information you want to record about each child with a brief note, on a Brief Notes Recording Sheet (see Appendix A). Some of the choices might include the following: pays attention to the story being read; stays through the entire story; responds to the teacher's questions; interacts in the story-reading experience with related ideas and comments. Watch the vignette or observe the story time, and make note of the first initial of each child's name (their names will appear by their faces during the vignette) by the brief note about that child. Do not worry about complete sentences or descriptive phrases. Try to be efficient in your use of words. Still remember to be factual and descriptive, not interpretive.

Group Discussion: Share some of the brief notes recorded by the group. Discuss the ease or difficulty of trying this type of documentation. How practical is such a recording method for your setting?

Reflection

Purpose: To reflect on what methods of documentation are effective in your setting

What to Do: Think about your work setting. Which of the following times will realistically work best for you to fit in observing and writing down what you are seeing?

- In the moment with the child
- As soon as possible after the event

- Stepping out of the action in teamwork with your colleagues
- In reflection

Will you combine some? How will you work with your colleagues to figure out what's best for your setting?

Finding Your Observation Style

Purpose: To determine what kind of documentation best fits your observation style

What to Do: Keep a record in your journal of your experience with each of the kinds of documentation methods we've discussed: running records, summative anecdotes, lists, the Quick Check and Brief Notes Recording Sheets. Which ones appeal to your own style of teaching, organization, observation, and writing? Why?

chapter 4

Preschool Choice
(may be used to tally one child's choices ...)

Date __Feb. 10__

Child(ren) ____

Art

Social/Emotion...

11 mins

...nipulatives

Sc...

...mins.

0

How Do You Observe for Assessment?

As you learn to focus your observations and become more adept at figuring out how to fit observation and documentation into your days with the children, you will find that you see children's development in action more clearly and more often. Your written records and your reflection on what you are seeing will help you communicate more effectively to others about a child. You will be able to show how well a child is doing and to identify possible areas of weakness or delay in his development, as well as how you and your colleagues are planning your curriculum to meet his needs. Parents, community members, and policy makers want evidence of the positive impact of early education and care on young children. Using observation for assessment is an authentic, child-friendly way to provide the evidence for such accountability.

Remember that assessing a child does not mean the same thing as testing a child. Specialists in early childhood education define assessment as a two-step process:

Diana: *I have taught preschool for thirty-five years and always done observations. Now I see something happening and I think, 'Oh, that belongs in the reading and writing development part,' or 'Oh, that belongs in the physical development part,' or 'Oh, it belongs in two or three different areas.' And so I am more organized in how I observe.*

1. First you gather information about a child through observation, collection of work samples or photographs, parent interviews, and tests.
2. Then you use that information to make judgments about his characteristics and decisions about appropriate teaching and care for him. (NAEYC and NAECS/SDE 2003)

Notice that tests are only one of several ways to gather the information. The problem with relying too heavily on testing is that the younger the child, the less reliable the test information becomes. You probably have recognized that young children do not follow directions well, and they don't complete paper and pencil tasks easily. Observation of a child performing actual tasks gives a truer picture of his capabilities. It is an "authentic measure"—one that reflects children's real-world performance, rather than their performance in contrived, adult-determined tasks that may be unfamiliar to them. Having appealing, hands-on activities in a familiar setting helps the child feel comfortable and relaxed, and his manipulation of objects, demonstration of concepts, and use of vocabulary will more accurately reflect what he can do. Observing over time provides opportunities for you to witness the frequency of the child's performance and evaluate whether the skill is truly in his repertoire, just emerging, or not there yet.

The word "assess" comes from the Latin verb *assidere,* which means "to sit with." In an assessment you "sit with" the learner. It is something you do *with* and *for* the child, not something you do *to* the child (Wiggins 1993 in Marzano and Kendall 1996). Too often in this present-day world of accountability and high-stakes evaluation in the public schools, standardized tests with quantitative results are used to pass or fail children. The importance of "sitting with" a child and observing what he can do has been lost. Assessment has come to be interpreted as determining if a child is performing up to a standard or grade level and, if not, blaming the program for failing to educate the child properly (Kohn 2000).

In the field of early childhood education, professional recommendations have emphasized returning to the original meaning of the word "assessment," "sitting with" a child in order to observe her and learn what she can do. In Appendix B we have included recommendations from position papers from national organizations such as the National Association for the Education of Young Children (NAEYC) and others regarding the best ways to assess young children. In addition, a glossary of terms related to different types of assessment is included. We hope that this information will give you a strong foundation of support for using observation as the primary way you collect information to assess children's development.

How Do Young Children Show What They Know and Can Do?

If tests are not the way that young children show their accomplishments, how do they show what they can and can't do?

- through their play
- by going about their daily routines
- by participating in teacher-designed activities

You observe them in these different situations in order to see how they demonstrate their skills, understanding of concepts, and general development.

Play

Through play children are continuously involved in clarifying and extending their understanding of the world, learning new concepts, and rethinking already known concepts. An infant plays with her toes or responds in babbles and squeals as she is bounced on your knee. Classic games such as peekaboo and patty-cake are ways in which you engage infants in play, helping them to learn about object permanence and fine motor control. Toddlers stack up a few blocks and knock them down over and over again, experimenting with their ability to manipulate and balance objects. As they play they are also learning about the consistency of gravity. With activity boards they push buttons and turn knobs to make sounds and feel the competence that comes from bringing about a predictable result. Young preschoolers imitate typical daily life in the house corner, integrating what they know about families and household tasks. Older preschoolers take their experiences into more complex play, planning a camping trip with set roles and use of a variety of materials to represent the needed camping supplies. Play consumes most of the waking hours of children in early childhood and increases in complexity as children grow and develop.

Play also reflects the cultural and social understanding of each child, enabling you to have a clearer picture of the influences on each child's activities and behaviors. For example, each child's representation of family life in house play will reflect the values, traditions, and heritage in which she is being raised. Play themes that are developed by the children help them to sustain play for ever-increasing periods of time, developing their ability to attend to a task. When you watch children playing in ways that are of interest to them, you see more. You get to know children on a deeper level.

Daily Routines

The times when preschoolers are washing their hands, preparing for snack, joining in large group time, and putting on coats to go outside can all be opportunities for you to observe children and learn more about them. Observing infants and toddlers as they separate from their parents at drop-off or watching them at feeding, diapering, and nap times can contribute information to your assessment process. As children go about their daily routines you learn much about their capabilities, their growing independence, their sense of self, and their general personalities. Cultural differences and family approaches to routines also become evident.

Teacher-Designed Activities

Observing children participating in teacher-designed activities will help you learn more about their development and will guide you in planning other activities for them. Designing specific activities for the children is an important part of being an early educator. Sometimes you choose certain materials for them. You may give your toddlers pudding to paint with at their high chairs. Or you may give your preschoolers rice and beans to measure. You may work with a small group of children with a task that is focused on a cognitive skill such as matching colors or recognizing their names. You may relate the activity to the interest of the children, making a counting game with bird stickers to go along with the children's interest in the bird house on your playground. When you are observing children in any of the above situations, you can observe for their specific developmental accomplishments in the cognitive, physical, social, and emotional areas. You can also watch them to determine what traits of more general cognitive stages or social-emotional competencies they are showing.

Robin: *A lot of times my co-teacher and I plan activities based on a concept that we want to see. So, for example, if we wanted to see children's cognitive level or skill as far as matching, we might pull out a matching game. We might actually strategize and have an activity planned ahead of time, and invite all of the children to do a small group game with us so that we can see where we are as a group and individually. And it really does help. Then we can talk about it after the children leave.*

Observing for Children's Cognitive Stages

Jean Piaget theorized that young children learn by constructing knowledge for themselves in interactions with the physical world and with other children. He identified important cognitive developmental tasks that children are working on during the early childhood years and emphasized that they need ample time to practice and integrate cognitive concepts (Labinowicz 1980).

- For infants and toddlers (ages birth to two) he named the developmental stage *sensori-motor.* Exploration and direct encounter with objects and others are the primary cognitive tasks. The focus of learning for the child is physical. Children are learning through their senses.

- For preschoolers (ages three to five) he called the developmental stage *preoperational,* with dramatic play, representation through language, and creating as the primary tasks.

Here are two descriptions of children at play. The first child is a toddler, the second a preschooler. Read the anecdotes and decide which Piagetian stage the children are demonstrating. What are their primary cognitive tasks as evidenced in their behavior and interactions?

> Wally (2 yrs. 5 mos.)
> During water play Wally runs toward the table, wobbling quickly from his left foot to his right. His face is bright and energetic, and he is smiling with his mouth slightly open. With a loud cooing noise, he quickly and abruptly approaches the water table. Something else catches his attention; he stops, spins around, and wobbles to a large, floor-length mirror on the wall. As he reaches it, he raises both arms high and allows them to slam upon the mirror as his entire body leans forward. Smiling at himself, he again produces a loud scream. Still smiling, he turns around, and with his arms still up above his head he relaxes his body and elatedly falls like a rag doll to the floor. (Klein, Wirth, and Linas 2003, 5)

> Daniel (4 yrs. 10 mos.)
> Daniel chooses to go to Dramatic Play and play post office. He puts on the mail carrier's uniform. Another child is dressed up as the mail carrier and has the mailbag. Daniel stands at the counter to give out stamps. He tells two children to be the mom and the dad. They start playing behind the counter with the stamps. "You're supposed to be the mom and the dad. Hey, you're supposed to be the mom and the dad. Hey, Teacher, I'm trying to tell them to be the mom and the dad." He starts pushing Trejo, who is holding

the mailbag, out from behind the counter. Daniel's voice is raised. "Hey, you're not supposed to be the worker. I'm the worker." Teacher starts to intervene as they both start to push each other. She asks Daniel, "What's going on?" "He's not the worker, and he's not supposed to be here." She asks, "What is he doing?" "He's trying to get here. He's trying to be the worker." She says, "Did you ask him what he wanted to be, or did you just tell him what to do?" Daniel changes his tone of voice, making it softer, not yelling. "Hey, do you want to be the worker?" Trejo says "No." Daniel says, "Then you pick up the mail. I'm the worker." Trejo takes off the mailbag and says he doesn't want to do that. Daniel picks it up. "Okay, I'm going to pick up the mail. You be the worker." They trade positions.

Wally is very clearly approaching the world through physical knowing, at the sensori-motor stage. He is playing with his environment, looking at the mirror, and experimenting with his own body. Daniel has moved to representational play, improvising and acting out his understanding of postal workers and post offices. Therefore, he is at the preoperational stage.

Watching children and identifying their cognitive stages can help you meet them at their level and plan activities that work well with the important cognitive tasks they are engaged in at that stage. A toddler at the sensori-motor stage is not interested in making a drawing or painting look like something—instead he is only interested in the texture and feel of the paint or the flow of the marker or chalk on the paper. He is paying attention to the process and the sensory information. A preschooler who is in the preoperational stage may be ready to try drawing and painting actual objects and will probably enjoy the process of doing so. Assessing the child's cognitive stage will help you better match activities and expectations so the child experiences success.

It will also help you figure out how much you can challenge the child to move ahead in her skills. Lev Vygotsky wrote that children's learning takes place in a *zone of proximal development* (also called a ZPD)—a zone in which they do not quite have the skills to be completely successful but with support may very well be able to perform (Berk and Winsler 1995). Observing to figure out each child's ZPD will help you be ready to support the child's growth. You will be less likely to overwhelm the child with activities that are too challenging. Instead, you will be providing just the right amount of challenge for each child.

Observing for Children's Social/Emotional Competencies

A major part of young children's lives is the development of their social and emotional competency. Erik Erikson (Erikson 1963) identified sequential stages in this process.

- *Trust* The first important task is the development of trust and connection to other human beings.
- *Autonomy* As trust is established, a child is then able to separate and be autonomous from the all-important base of love and connection that has been formed with his parents or primary caregivers.
- *Initiative* Preschoolers are learning to use their own ideas to think about and understand the world around them. Initiative is important for young children's healthy personality development. Their imaginative play is the way for them to act on their ideas, thoughts, and concerns. When encouraged and supported by the adults in their lives, children work on developing competence and on mastering their world.

Observing children's behavior in daily routines as well as in play episodes can help you determine their stage of social/emotional competency. Observing for a child's sense of trust, autonomy, and initiative gives you more insight into that child's approach to the world. A child who is untrusting in your setting will not try new things or take risks. You may find it hard to learn more about her cognitive capabilities because she hesitates to play with the sorting materials or read a book with you. The first step is building a relationship with her so that she can relax, feel more comfortable in your program, and start showing you what she can do. Some children who have lots of initiative may seem hard to deal with. They are rowdy, high energy, and confident about their own capabilities. Recognizing that their sense of mastery of their world is strong may help you and your colleagues see them in a different light and figure out ways to channel their energy.

Read the following anecdotes, and identify the ways in which the children are working on the development of trust, autonomy, or initiative. What are they learning to master?

> **Kaelin (2 yrs. 0 mos.)**
> Kaelin's parents are out of town, so he got dropped off at school in the morning by his grandparents. As the grandparents were leaving, the teacher held Kaelin. He then gave her a hug. The grandparents said, "Have a good day." Kaelin blew them a kiss good-bye. He cried a little while and continued to hug the teacher.

> **Paul (5 yrs. 2 mos.)**
> Today during outside time Paul is in the sandbox digging with a friend. "See what we're doing, Debbie?" Paul asks me. He continues to dig and says, "We're raking the holes for the prairie dogs. Want to fill it up?" Paul asks his friend. His friend says, "Sure." Paul continues to talk to his friend. "These are very easy holes. We're digging very deep holes." He pats his bucket with sand and says, "There we go." As Paul digs a little more, he says with a great big smile and eyes wide open, "Hey, I can see the bottom of the sandbox!"

Kaelin is developing trust and autonomy. He is able to separate from loved ones, although with some tears, and be comforted by his caregivers. Paul is showing initiative and accomplishment. He follows through with his plan to rake, fill up, and dig. His excitement in digging to the bottom is evident.

Sometimes analyzing the types of play you observe children engaging in will help you learn more about the social experiences of each child. You may see children engage in any of the following types of play:

- *Solitary Play* Toddlers begin to play on their own independently of others.
- *Onlooker Play* Toddlers watch others playing, showing an interest but not entering into the play.
- *Parallel Play* As the child becomes more aware of others, he may start to play alongside other children without really interacting. This is seen in older toddlers as well as preschoolers.
- *Associative Play* During the preschool years, children's play becomes more connected to other children. They want to interact and create play episodes with others. You may see children playing with others, but the play is random, not seeming to have an organized plan among the players.
- *Cooperative Play* In this stage two or more children have a play theme that they are developing. The sense of togetherness is very strong. Children are performing specific and scripted roles in the play. This type of play is the precursor of organized games with rules that emerge in middle childhood.

You can observe children's play in order to identify which of these types you are seeing. In the video vignettes accompanying this book are several scenes that show children demonstrating various types of play. Hunter watches the other toddlers at the water table before he joins in, thus demonstrating onlooker play. Alex and Matthew build with blocks alongside each other, imitating each other's structures and interacting verbally ("Look at mine, Alex"), but not joining together in a play script or theme. Their play may be seen as parallel or associative play. Look at the following anecdote, and decide what type of play these children are engaging in.

> Sophie (4 yrs. 2 mos.), Nicholas (4 yrs. 7 mos.),
  Issy (3 yrs. 10 mos.), Nina (5 yrs.)
  "Go get us some muffins, and we'll jump into the car," Sophie orders
  Nicholas as she and Issy run hand in hand to the slide. Beneath the slope
  of the slide their car awaits them, as well as their plan for a getaway. Soon
  after, Nicholas comes running back, his hands held out in front of him.
  "Here are the muffins," he says as he hands both Sophie and Issy a piece of
  warm, buttered air. "I'll drive," he says, as he skootches into the driver's
  seat just below the foot of the slide. Nicholas positions his feet in front of
  him, bends his knees, and places his hands in front of him as if he's gripping
  a steering wheel. Sophie and Issy wiggle backward to accommodate their
  friend, as they spread their legs around one another and place their hands
  on the shoulders of the child in front of them—a three-child chain. "Can
  I hop in?" yells Nina just before the car slips away. "Sure!" hollers Sophie.
  "Hop in back." And Nina quickly crawls into the back seat—one of the
  compartments of this plastic playground. And they're off, off to the sound
  of Nicholas's revved-up engine.
     Then it's cleanup time, and the pizza man enters the stage. "Who
  ordered a pepperoni pizza?" Sophie hollers as she carries a block toward
  the block shed. "I did," returns Nicholas, as he takes the large wooden
  block from Sophie and places it into the shed. He has assigned himself the
  role of block organizer for the day, and he neatly stacks the wooden pizzas
  according to size. And soon the chant is echoed through the class as they
  pass the blocks to Nicholas: "Who ordered a cheese pizza?" "Here's a pizza!"
  And soon enough the blocks are neatly stacked in the shed. (Klein, Wirth,
  and Linas 2003, 1)

Sophie, Nicholas, Issy, and Nina are involved in cooperative play, using their imaginations to spontaneously develop play scripts regarding muffins, driving, and pizza delivery. Notice how cleanup of the blocks got accomplished in the meantime!

Observing to Assess Children's Specific Developmental Skills

When you observe children, you can assess the broader areas of cognitive and social/emotional competencies, or you can look closely at specific developmental skills in the cognitive, physical, social, and emotional developmental areas. Within each of these areas, children demonstrate their capabilities in different ways.

- You see cognitive capabilities in how they
  - communicate their wants and needs
  - go about solving problems
  - explore and understand their world
  - as preschoolers, develop their understanding of math, science, and literacy concepts
- You see physical capabilities in how they
  - use their large muscles to move and coordinate their bodies (often referred to as gross motor development)
  - use the smaller muscles of their hands to manipulate objects and tools (often referred to as fine motor development)
- You see social and emotional capabilities in how they
  - show their personality traits
  - develop relationships with adults and peers
  - show their developing independence
  - respond to frustration and challenge
  - learn to regulate their own behavior

Children often show their specific skills in their play and participation in daily routines. You can also design special activities and provide materials so that you can observe for their capabilities in any of the areas listed above.

Think back to the observation in Chapter 1 about Angel during the everyday routine of snack. Remember that almost every major area of development was seen as Angel went about his snack routine. Read the following anecdote about JoAnngela. In this case the teacher invited JoAnngela and two other children to read a story with her. This is an example of observing a child's performance in a teacher-designed activity. As you read the observation, determine what you are learning about what JoAnngela can do. Then identify the developmental areas and specific skills contained in the observation.

> JoAnngela (3 yrs. 8 mos.)
JoAnngela, Damien, and Adrianne sit down with me to read <u>The Three Little Pigs</u>. JoAnngela sits for a while listening to the story. About halfway through the story, she gets on her knees and begins to rock back and forth. She bumps into Damien and tells him, "Sorry, Damien." She then stands up, moves to the other side of Adrianne, curls up on the beanbag, and finishes listening to the story.

Using the list of the major areas of child development in analyzing the observation about JoAnngela, you can see evidence to support conclusions about JoAnngela's capabilities in all of the developmental areas.

- *Cognitive Development* Problem-solves by moving herself around during the story and stays with the task so that she listens to a whole story; uses language to communicate with another child
- *Social Development* Bumps into a friend and apologizes
- *Emotional Development* Shows awareness of another child's feelings; comforts self by rocking and curling up
- *Physical Development* Sits, stands, and kneels

Here are two other examples of observation notes. One incident took place during feeding time, the other during work with puzzles provided by the teacher. Read each note, and determine what you are learning that the child can do. Then identify what developmental areas and specific skills are contained in the observation.

> Elisha (7 mos.)
During lunch Elisha is sitting in a high chair being fed applesauce when she looks away from the spoon. I call her name, and she turns and babbles and smiles. She then continues to babble and look at me while being fed.

Here's what we learned about Elisha from this observation:

- *Cognitive Development* Responds to adult language, specifically her name, by looking and smiling; expresses her own language through babbling
- *Social Development* Interacts with the observer
- *Emotional Development* Smiles, showing trust in her caregiver
- *Physical Development* Sits in a high chair

> Gabriella (3 yrs. 8 mos.)
Gabriella is at the cash register, and there is a store set up. Another child comes over and picks up a fire hat. Gabriella says, "The fire hat is 89, 88, 88, 88, and that's all." While she is saying this, she is writing on her tablet.

She gives the other child some money from the cash register and says, "This says that will be two moneys." She then writes more and says, "I will write 'Gabriella' right here."

Here's what we learned about Gabriella from this observation:

- *Cognitive Development* Engages in pretend play imitating the world around her; uses language to communicate with another child; imitates writing as purposeful
- *Social Development* Engages in play with another child
- *Emotional Development* Appears to be confident and self-motivated in her play and interactions
- *Physical Development* Uses fine motor skills to write

Observing for All Areas of Development

Your goal is to collect information about each child in all areas: cognitive, physical, social, and emotional. You can do that through observations that are more general, like those above, or ones that are focused on specific skills. Sometimes you find that you observe a child with a focus on a specific area. You may want to capture how the child is using language to communicate with others or how the child shows her growing skills in gross motor coordination. You and your colleagues choose a focus and plan for your observations. Here are two examples of more focused observation notes. For Jesus, his teachers were watching closely for his developing social skills. For Genevieve, the focus was on her problem-solving skills.

> Jesus (2 yrs. 2 mos.)
> During free play Jesus pushes Angel in a toy car. Jesus pushes him into another child, and the other child falls on the ground and begins to cry. Jesus runs to the other child, hugs him while still on the floor, then babbles something to him, and helps him get up. The other child stops crying, and they each resume their play.

What did we learn about Jesus's developing social skills?
- *Social Development* Plays with another child and shows empathy

> Genevieve (3 yrs. 4 mos.)
> Genevieve is playing with beans that are in the dry water table. She fills up the bucket and then dumps it out a number of times. She fills smaller containers, trying to get more and more beans into the container. She then

tries pouring beans from a tablespoon into a teaspoon and then back
and forth. She occasionally puts the beans down while trying to get more
beans into the small container.

What did we learn about Genevieve's problem-solving skills?

- *Problem Solving* Solves problems through observation,
  hands-on trial and error, and repetition

Sometimes what gets written down about a child shows what the
teacher was paying the most attention to or what he was most concerned about for that child. If teachers don't take care to keep track
of which developmental areas have been observed, some areas may
be missed and others overemphasized. Children's behavior can sometimes influence what gets recorded, especially when difficulties arise.
The following observation was presented as a focused documentation
of the child's math skills. Does it include any information about the
child's math skills? You be the judge.

> Jay (4 yr. 10 mos.)
  Jay does not sit in his seat at the math table. Instead, he jumps up out of
  his chair or lies across the table. He does not participate in the counting
  activity. He stacks the counters in a pile, and then knocks it down and laughs.

This anecdote does not include any information about Jay's math
skills, does it? Instead, it describes Jay's behavior during a math activity.
Certainly his behavior is a concern. And interventions should be tried
to help him attend to the task at hand and participate in the counting
activity. However, special attention should also be paid to gathering
information about Jay's counting capabilities (or other mathematical
understandings) in a variety of activities so that this important area of
his development is not left out of the observation record. Perhaps Jay
is keenly aware of who is first and second in line each day. Or maybe he
helps to count how many children are present and absent each morning. Having Jay help set the table and recording how he goes about
matching one cup, one napkin, and one plate to each chair would give
evidence of his growing one-to-one correspondence.

Looking over the observation notes you have written for each child,
you should see notes about all areas of development. For a preschooler
such as Jay, those notes would include observations of his behavior,
math and problem-solving skills, language, socialization, early literacy,
creative development, and fine and gross motor skills. For an infant or

toddler, observations would focus on their separation from their family members, attachment to care providers, capabilities at comforting themselves and getting their emotional and physical needs met, and skills in exploring their environment.

Observing and documenting children's behavior is an important part of assessing their social and emotional development. It can be difficult to write a factual description when a child is misbehaving, but it is important to do so. Taking a deep breath and waiting to write until you calm down and have a chance to reflect on what happened will help you stay objective as you describe what the child said and did, and include what interventions you and your colleagues provided. In Chapter 5 we will look more closely at ways to use observation to learn what might be behind children's behavior and deal with it more effectively.

Tying Observations to Developmental Checklists or Resources

To determine the age level of a child's capabilities in the cognitive, physical, social, and emotional areas, you turn to developmental checklists or resources that specify reasonable expectations for children at different ages. A variety of sources are available.

The following includes information for infants and toddlers only:

■ *The Ounce Scale* (Meisels et al. 2003)

The following provide information for children from birth through age five:

■ *Developmentally Appropriate Practice, from the National Association for the Education of Young Children* (Bredekamp and Copple 1996)

■ *Developmental Milestones Charts in Focused Portfolios: A Complete Assessment for the Young Child* (Gronlund and Engel 2001). These are based on the information from NAEYC above.

■ *The Assessment, Evaluation, and Programming System (AEPS) for Infants and Children* (Bricker 1997)

The following include information for children from age three to five:

■ *The Creative Curriculum Developmental Continuum* (does include forerunners to three-year-old expectations) (Dodge, Colker, and Heroman 2002)

■ *The High/Scope Child Observation Record* (High/Scope 1992)

This source covers the range from preschool (age three) through fifth grade:

■ *The Work Sampling System Developmental Guidelines* (Marsden et al. 1994)

Other possibilities exist as well. All of these sources give information about age-appropriate expectations in various developmental areas. Some of the sources are more specific than others. Some are formatted along a continuum. Others include a checklist or computerized recording sheet. In addition, these sources were all designed in such a way as to allow for cultural and socioeconomic differences among children's performance. The goal is that the developmental information is not biased toward any one group. All of these checklists and charts are designed to be used as ways to evaluate observations of children in action. You observe the child, write the observation down, and then at some point relate it back to the developmental checklist or resource to determine the level of the child's performance.

Here are some examples of how teachers related their observations to developmental sources in order to identify children's developmental capabilities.

The Work Sampling System

Pam and Linda, a preschool teaching team, met at the end of one week to plan for the next. As part of the planning discussion, they reflected about what they saw children doing in teacher-led activities as well as child-initiated exploration. Pam noted that many of the children had been participating in block play and combining that play with extensive pretend scripts about pirates and ships and hidden treasure. Children had used the largest wooden blocks to create a large pirate ship with a car steering wheel at the helm. Various dress-up clothes and hats were incorporated as children took on different roles within the play. Pam and Linda laughed as they remembered some of the language the children used as they negotiated about the actions of the pirates, and the enthusiasm they showed as they shouted, "Ahoy, matey!"

Pam and Linda had written down their observations on notepads. As they read through and discussed their documentation, they realized that they were learning much about the children's abilities. They turned to the developmental checklist their program used, *The Work Sampling System Preschool-4 Developmental Guidelines*. As they looked over the checklist, they concluded that they had observational evidence to mark individual children's performance in the following checklist items:

- Approach to Learning: Performance Indicator C.3. "Approaches tasks with flexibility and inventiveness."
- Interaction with Others: Performance Indicator D.1. "Interacts easily with one or more children, beginning to work or play cooperatively."
- Speaking: Performance Indicator B.2. "Uses language for a variety of purposes."
- Gross Motor Development: Performance Indicator A.1. "Moves with enough balance and control to perform simple, large motor tasks."

Pam and Linda thought carefully about the group of children they had observed and marked each child's checklist according to his or her participation and interactions around the pirate play. The choices for marks on *The Work Sampling System Preschool-4 Developmental Guidelines* include "not yet," "in process," and "proficient." For Mario, who took great leadership in the organization and building of the pirate ship and helped determine the roles and script of the pirate play, they marked "proficient" in all of the indicators identified earlier. For Alicia, who watched the play from afar and then joined in when Mario gave her specific directions and did not verbalize much during the play, they marked "in process" for most of the indicators. Pam and Linda were very careful to think about each child's participation clearly in the dramatic play they witnessed. And they decided to focus more closely on this dramatic play in the next week so that they could collect even more evidence of the children's performance in these areas.

The Assessment, Evaluation, and Programming System (AEPS)

Sarah and Juanita decided to watch their two-year-olds with a focus on their fine motor skills. They used *The Assessment, Evaluation, and Programming System (AEPS)* for Infants and Children to identify reasonable expectations of children's developmental accomplishments. In the Fine Motor Domain, they found that in Strand A, "Reach, Grasp, and Release," this was Goal 4: "Grasps pea-size object with either hand using tip of the index finger and thumb with hand and/or arm *not* resting on surface for support." In Strand B, "Functional Use of Fine Motor Skills," this was Goal 2 : "Assembles toy and/or object that require(s) putting pieces together."

In order to observe children in action demonstrating these two goals, they planned to serve Cheerios and raisins for snack and watch as the children used their pincer grasps to pick up the small pieces. With their clipboards and pens at the ready while the children ate snack, Sarah and Juanita made notes about each child's efforts toward picking up the Cheerios and raisins. After snack they put out large lacing beads and strings, and several knob puzzles on tables, and they sat with the children, again with clipboards in hand so that they could make note of children's abilities to string the beads and place the puzzle pieces. After the children left for the day, they recorded the results of their observations regarding these two goals on the *AEPS* Data Recording Forms for each child. The markings for scoring include the following:

2	Pass consistently
1	Inconsistent performance
0	Does not pass

Qualifying Notes are made on the forms as well and include the following:

A	Assistance Provided
B	Behavior interfered
R	Reported assessment
M	Modification/adaptation
D	Direct test

Sarah and Juanita carefully considered how each child had gone about showing his or her fine motor capabilities and rated each child accordingly on the *AEPS* forms.

Focused Portfolios

One afternoon after the children had left, as Carol, Phil, and Kissee cleaned up the classroom, they discussed how their three- to five-year-olds had listened so well to the *Pancakes* story that day. They remembered that certain children had been more verbally engaged in telling the story and responding to Carol's questions. But at the end of the day it was hard to remember exactly which children said what. They realized that they needed to be prepared to focus on children's responses when stories were read, so they decided to have documentation materials available for whichever adult was not reading the story aloud to the children. In this way the details of children's listening skills, reading comprehension, and interest in stories would not be missed. They figured that even if a child was sitting on a lap, that teacher could still write some brief notes down as his or her colleague led the story experience.

Their program had adopted *Focused Portfolios* as their assessment process and used the developmental milestones charts from the *Focused Portfolios* book as the source of developmental expectations for the children. As Carol, Phil, and Kissee thought about documenting the children's interest in and interactions with a story experience, they planned to use the *Focused Portfolios* Developmental Milestones Collection Forms to record their observations. They placed several of the forms on a clipboard and brought this clipboard along with a pen to the next large group time when a story was being read.

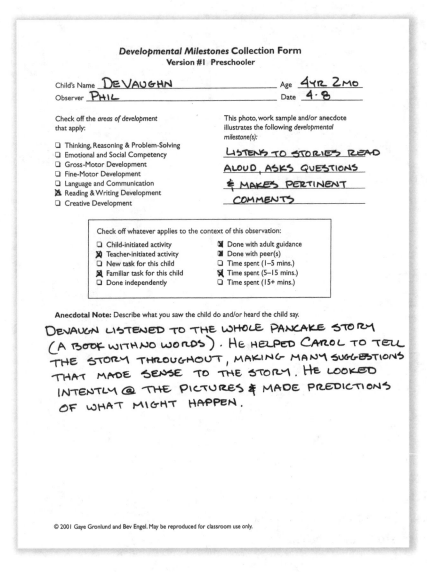

Here is an example of a form that shows an observation of one of their children in a story experience. Note that the *Focused Portfolios* Developmental Milestones Collection Form includes additional information pertinent to the observation: the date, the child's age, the observer's name, and the developmental area and milestones that are evidenced in this observation. Using this format, Carol, Phil, and Kissee wrote out the anecdote as they observed the child in action. Then they went back after observing (at a break in the action, at snack or naptime, or after the children left for the day) and filled out the developmental information included on the top part of the form.

Choosing a Source and Identifying the Documentation Process

The staff and administration of every early childhood program choose a developmental reference that best suits the needs of their setting. Some state or federally funded programs are told which checklist or assessment system is to be used for accountability purposes. Funding as well as program evaluation may be tied to the results of such assessments. If such mandates are not in place, you and your colleagues should review various checklists and charts to determine which best suits your understanding of child development. It is also important for you to consider the process of documenting and organizing your observations and relating them back to the checklist or chart. Match both the source and the process to the education and experience of your staff, to the realities of your day-to-day work with young children, and to the ways in which you want to communicate the information to your families. This way you can be sure that the specific observational assessment tool gets used in the most effective manner.

In addition, when choosing your source of developmental information, you have a responsibility to make sure that the milestones identified are reflective of the cultural variation of the children and families in your program. Again, the ones noted earlier in this chapter have been developed to be valid across cultures, races, and socioeconomic levels. Here is a story from an early educator who was asked to use an assessment reference tool that was not appropriate for the cultural setting in which she worked.

> *I worked for an early intervention agency dealing with children ages birth to three. The agency had an agreement to provide developmental screenings for a western Native American tribe. As we assessed the children in the Early Head Start Program, we found that, without exception, every child came out with speech and language concerns and a referral for further testing or for speech therapy. Many of the children also showed "cognitive delays," according to the screening. I began to question these results and discovered that many Native people use many gestures to communicate with their children, especially when they are very young. Many of the children were also being raised to be bilingual. They communicated in two languages. Another issue was that children who are not highly verbal often do not do well on developmental screens in the area of cognitive development because they don't respond to the questions. I remember how appalled I was when the psychologist would show*

the child a picture of a giraffe and ask them what it was. If you asked any of the children what an antelope or an elk was, they would surely know. I began to realize that the assessment tool we were using had been developed and normed on white, middle-class children and was not relevant to the culture of the tribe.

In this case, the conclusions drawn about the children based on this child development information were not accurate reflections of their actual performance and capabilities.

The following is a suggested set of criteria for evaluating developmental resources and checklists. You can easily add any other relevant criteria as you review resources and discuss them with your colleagues.

Evaluation of Developmental Resources & Checklists

Name of assessment tool: _____

Evaluation criteria:

- Number of milestones or indicators appears reasonable _____

- Milestones or indicators make sense

  and apply to what I know about young children _____

- Looks easy to learn _____

- Is culturally inclusive _____

- Looks easy to use _____

- Is family friendly and informative _____

- Is cost-effective _____

- Other _____

  _____

Your director or supervisor can borrow or order one copy of each of several observational assessments. Then a team from your program can review them, using the above criteria. In this way you can choose a checklist or chart that will match the needs of your program, children, families, and staff.

An excellent resource to turn to for review of a variety of observational assessments is *Linking Assessment and Early Intervention: An Authentic Curriculum-Based Approach* (Bagnato, Neisworth, and Munson 1997). In this book fifty-two curriculum-based assessment instruments, systems, and procedures are reviewed and rated. Each description includes ordering and pricing information, as well as the following:

- Assessment type
- Age/focus group
- Scale(s)
- Data system
- Domain/content
- Special needs options
- Authenticity
- Family involvement
- Training needed
- Validation
- Comments

This book can be a helpful and time-saving start to the review process. However, it is missing some of the newer versions of assessment tools (such as *The Creative Curriculum Developmental Continuum*) and newer approaches (such as *Focused Portfolios* or *The Ounce Scale*). It should not be considered the only source of review information, then, but it can certainly provide helpful ways of evaluating many observational assessment systems and designs.

Practice Making Developmental Connections

Here are some anecdotes of children in action along with portions of developmental checklists and milestones charts from a variety of assessments. First read the anecdote. Then determine how you would mark the child's developmental capabilities based on the developmental information from each source.

> Haley (3 yrs. 6 mos.)
> The gymnastics teacher's son is at gym class today. I notice Haley walking close by him. She then comes up to tell me, "Hey, Laura, I 'hi' to him." She then points up to the ceiling where a ball is stuck between boards and says, "Hey, look. Pink up there."

Using the following developmental resources, how would you rate Haley's language performance?

Preschool Developmental Milestones Chart

	24 months to 3 years	Three-Year-Old Level	Four-Year-Old Level	Five-Year-Old Level
Language & Communication	combines words	vocabulary increasing steadily, using sentences of at least 3 or 4 words to express wants and needs	talks to others about personal acquaintances, experiences, and acquisitions (in small and large groups)	uses complex sentence structure, and has the vocabulary to express most wants, needs, and explanations, without difficulty
	listens to short stories (one-on-one and in small groups)	begins to listen and attend to others	listens to others and tries to participate in conversation	participates actively in conversations, listening attentively and with patience to others' contributions
	speaking vocabulary may reach 200 words	learns words to simple finger plays, rhymes, and songs, especially those with a lot of repetition and hand motions	restates multi-step directions	can follow multi-step instructions and requests
	plays pretend using sounds and words	can tell a simple story, often focusing only on favorite parts	can retell the basic sequence of a story	remembers and recites poems, songs, and story and movie sequences, and acts them out
	uses compound sentences		uses some positional words (e.g., under, over, on)	uses positional words (e.g., under, over, on)
	recounts events of the day			
	uses adjectives and adverbs			

From the *High/Scope* Child Observation Record

Child does not yet speak or uses only a few one- or two-word phrases	Child uses simple sentences of more than two words	Child uses sentences that include two or more separate ideas	Child uses sentences that include two or more ideas with descriptive details ("I stacked up the red blocks too high, and they fell down")	Child makes up and tells well-developed, detailed stories, rhymes, or songs

From *The Creative Curriculum Developmental Continuum*

Curriculum Objective	Forerunners	I	II	III
Expresses self using words and expanded sentences	Uses non-verbal gestures or single words to communicate, e.g., *points to ball;* uses 2-word phrases, e.g., *"All gone," "go out"*	Uses simple sentences (3–4 words) to express wants and needs, e.g., *"I want the trike."*	Uses longer sentences (5–6 words) to communicate, e.g., *"I want to ride the trike when we go outside."*	Uses more complex sentences to express ideas and feelings, e.g., *"I hope we can go outside today because I want to ride the tricycle around the track."*

> Anthony (3 yrs. 8 mos.)
> Anthony puts a new puzzle on the table and says he is going to make it by himself. He takes one piece at a time and turns and presses until he finds the correct place for the piece. The puzzle has eight small pieces. He does this with no assistance. He turns the last piece and finishes the puzzle.

Use the following developmental resources to assess Anthony's development.

From *The Work Sampling System* Preschool-3 Developmental Guidelines		
Personal and Social Development		
Self Concept		
2. Starts to show self-direction in action	**Rating:**	
	Not Yet	
	In Process	
	Proficient	
Physical Development		
Fine Motor Development		
2. Uses eye-hand coordination to perform tasks	**Rating:**	
	Not Yet	
	In Process	
	Proficient	

From the *AEPS*					
Fine Motor Domain					
Functional use of fine motor skills					
2. Assembles toys/objects that require putting pieces together	**Scoring Key:**			**Qualifying Notes:**	
2.2. Fits object into defined space	2 = Pass consistently			A = Assistance provided	
	1 = Inconsistent performance			B = Behavior interfered	
	0 = Does not pass			R = Reported assessment	
				M = Modification/adaptation	
				D = Direct test	

Choosing an observational assessment tool or resource and implementing it successfully takes time, commitment to learning the system, and willingness to experiment with new ideas and change old ways. For many early educators, the learning curve may necessitate one or two years of training, implementation, and ongoing support before they feel comfortable with the new approach. Recognizing and planning for the time to discuss, share successes and challenges, and seek additional information and implementation ideas are important. Learning through trial and error brings long-term results. Working closely with colleagues to explore the best and most efficient ways to fit observation and documentation into busy days with children will create a more positive and helpful atmosphere.

Calls for accountability should be examined carefully so that all assessment processes are used to the benefit of the children, not to their detriment. Observing children in everyday classroom activities will provide more realistic and truthful evaluations of children's developmental capabilities than evaluations that come from contrived, occasional testing situations. Writing factual, descriptive anecdotes will ground observational assessment in the objective realm, rather than the subjective, judgmental one. Choosing reliable sources of developmental expectations that have been researched across cultures, regions, and economic levels will validate any conclusions drawn about the child's performance and help teachers make appropriate decisions about how best to support the child's continued growth.

How Do You Share Assessment Information with Families?

Early educators have a professional responsibility to communicate with families in supportive and meaningful ways and to ask for their thoughts and opinions regarding their child's care and education. Sharing what has been learned about their child's development through observation is an essential part of the process. It is through this process that you build a trusting and respectful relationship with families and truly work together for the benefit of the child.

Opening a dialogue with family members about their children can be a wonderfully enriching and meaningful experience. Sharing developmental information with families regarding their children and inviting them to share their joys and their concerns helps both parties to better understand and meet the needs of the children. Families have a unique perspective on their children, knowing them and understanding them in intimate ways that early educators do not. For infants, they know their sleeping and eating patterns. For toddlers, they can share their approach to toilet training. They can provide information about a child's interests and developmental capabilities that have not been seen during the time that the child is in care. They can share family traditions and unique cultural practices.

This addition of the family perspective can make the process of individualizing curriculum more effective for you. Sometimes family members see children doing things at home that they do not yet do while in your care. Children function differently in different settings. A quiet child at preschool may be a very talkative child at home. Learning this information helps you feel reassured about the child's language skills and helps you view her in a different light. Children may show more behavioral self-control at the child care program than they do in their home setting. Sharing this information can be reassuring to parents who are struggling with tantrums and disruption at home.

Both family members and early educators want children to thrive and be successful. Families also want to know that the program is having a positive impact on their child. They want the early childhood program staff to be accountable for their actions and to know that the goals of the program are reflected in the day-to-day activities with the children. They want to know how their child is doing, the activities that their child participates in, and what their child likes to do at school. They want to know what you see as far as their child's developmental and learning strengths. And they may worry about what you might identify as potential areas of concern. Having a special time to share with family members is another way to give them the message that their child is in good hands, with people who are helping him grow and learn. Assessments based on observation provide families with a caring and nonthreatening way to see their child's growth, development, and learning. By sharing descriptions of children in action throughout their days at the program, you are providing much more meaningful information to families than check sheets or report cards. You are giving them a window through which to see their child when she is away from home.

Choosing a Format for Reporting to Families

Once you have chosen a system for recording observations and a resource to interpret those observations and determine the child's developmental capabilities, you will want to decide upon a format for presenting the information to family members. These decisions are often made by the administrators and staff of a program. This provides consistency among all of the early educators in a program and helps

Focused Portfolios Reflection and Planning Form

Child's Name: Sydney Hovde   Age: 4 yrs 11 m   Teacher: Peggy   Date 5/4

Teacher Reflection
Refer to all areas of development and to the items in the portfolio

Summarize information from Favorites, Friends, and Family:
- Although Sydney stays in various areas of our facility, none capture her attention as fully as the art center. She often stays in the area most of the choice time before our circle.
- Sydney is happy to play with most of the children in our childcare. She really does not have a favorite person, but plays well with most all of them. She really does not make connections with Michael, Jayden or Logan.
- Sydney loves her family and interacts great with all of them. She is especially loving to her brother, protecting and helping him through the day. She loves the time during her daily routine of saying good bye to her mom and dad.

List milestones accomplished:
- Counts objects and refers to the quantity of items in talking about them
- Demonstrates interest in exploring aspects of home, school, and community
- Shows comfort with new people and situations and cooperates in group play and work time
- Hops, jumps and climbs well
- Uses scissors unassisted and shows phonemic awareness - symbol connections - beginning sounds
- Remembers and recites poems, songs, and stories and acts them out
- Writes using conventional words and names
- Explores a variety of expressive media with purpose, often with a product in mind

Describe progress that has been observed:
When Sydney started school this year, she was uncomfortable writing her name. Her letters were still somewhat crude, but readable by adults. When the art center became her favorite place, she started writing her name more and showing an interest in other letters, first her brother Sam's name. She continues to write, write, write. This led to more risk taking, which led to more complex writing. She now shows phonemic awareness with beginning sounds and being able to hear the sound in words.

List the milestones that this child is working on (these are the goals for the next collection):
- Demonstrates huge interest in exploring home, school, and community.
- Works hard to solve problems independently or with some adult coaching and support
- Pencil control forming letters
- "Reads" print in the environment

Family and Teacher Planning

Discuss plans to support further development. Write ideas for classroom activities, family involvement, and teacher support. Add any general comments.

Teacher:
- Sydney is very interested in all of our activities. She loves to use her hands, touching and still sometimes puts things in her mouth to "feel" that way. She loves to learn. I will continue to encourage Sydney to retell events in her life. As she retells, she becomes more aware of the event and how it panned out. This has greatly extended her vocabulary and language ability Although Sydney has great language, she still prefers to come and tell on the children when conflict arises, so I will continue to coach her when this happens.
- Sydney has progressed significantly in so many ways this year. Probably the biggest leap is in her use of the art center. She continues to spend a good amount of time there. As she dictates to me about her art projects, I am going to let her write the letters she knows in the words. I want to encourage her interest in print. I will continue to add new items into the art center.
- I am going to encourage Sydney to "read" our environment. I am going to make sure items of interest are labeled in our childcare.

It has been wonderful to observe Sydney this year. She brings her great language skills and her creativity to all areas where she chooses to work. We have enjoyed her tremendously.

Family member(s):

parents know what to expect as far as assessment information about their child. In some settings the decision is up to an individual teacher. Again, communicating clearly to parents is important. Dividing up the documentation in order to show what the child can do and what developmental skills are emerging or not evident helps family members understand their child's strengths and weaknesses. Setting goals to reflect on how you and your colleagues, as well as the family members, will work with the child is also part of the process.

Some observational assessment systems have reports for you to use when conferencing with families. *The Work Sampling System* and *The Creative Curriculum Developmental Continuum* have summary reports for evaluating and interpreting the observations of the child, as well as the checklist information that has been documented from those observations. Both of these systems recommend that teachers share these reports along with a few actual observations of the child and some examples of the child's performance in the form of photographs and work samples (paintings, drawings, writing samples, and so forth). *The Ounce Scale* has a parent portfolio for family members to document their own observations of their infant's or toddler's accomplishments of milestones. The *Focused Portfolios* approach to conferencing includes sharing observations written on specially designed collection forms, along with a Reflection and Planning Form to summarize and interpret the observations and the child's developmental capabilities. See an example of a completed Reflection and Planning Form on the previous page.

Some teachers create their own report form. For example, Diana Lamb at Little Lamb Nursery School uses the *Focused Portfolios* approach for organizing her observations, but she created the following format for reporting to family members.

Preparing for the Family Conference

No matter which system is being used, the beginning step in preparing for a family conference is reflection. Take the time to sit down and go through the documentation to determine the growth and learning that has occurred. This helps you to interpret the child's progress and identify areas of concern. Of course, the process of reflecting has been ongoing for you as the documentation has been collected. But before the conference it is time to stop collecting data and focus on what has been collected, making decisions as to what information is to be presented and fitting it to the chosen format. This can lead to new insights about a child.

Little Lamb Nursery School

Name_____ Date_____

Developmental Milestones

1. **Gross motor development**

   Active   Jumping   Hopping

2. **Fine motor development**

   Scissors   Drawing   Name
   Works Independently

3. **Emotional & Social competency**

   Type of play

   Relationship with others

   Self discipline

   Self image

   Self help skills

4. **Thinking, Reasoning, and Problem Solving**

   Number readiness

   Attention span

   Curious

   Generates ideas

5. **Language & Communication**

   Understands & Follows directions

   Participates in group conversation

   Vocabulary

6. **Creative Development**

   Art

   Music

   Dramatic play

7. **Reading and Writing Development**

   Listens to stories
   Interest in letters, books

General Comments about This Child's Growth And Development Over the Course of the Year

Teacher Reflections:

Describe progress observed:

Milestones this child is working on:

Family Member's Comments:

Scheduling Conferences in a Family-Friendly Way

Meetings with family members to share information should be scheduled regularly. Many programs schedule two or three specific times during the course of the year for teachers to meet with family members to discuss their child's development and learning. Most early childhood programs have information in their policies and procedures defining this expectation and alerting parents to the time frames involved. Casual meetings with family members, such as at arrival or pickup time, are important times for establishing relationships and for daily communication. But a more formal time for conferencing provides an opportunity for you and the family members to look in depth at the child's accomplishments and struggles and to figure out how to work together as partners in the best interest of the child.

It is imperative that the meeting be scheduled to meet the needs of the family and far enough in advance for them to make arrangements to attend. Too often families are not given flexibility and choice as to where and when to meet. Then the staff feels frustrated when families are not able to attend. Because of the unique needs of families, meeting times and places need to be individualized. Setting up a conference in the evening may be necessary, perhaps even at the family's home. Often breakfast or lunch meetings are successful for family members who are working outside of the home, either meeting in a restaurant or brown-bagging it at a convenient location. Some of the time phone conferencing is the only option. The difficulty with a phone call is that you cannot look at the observations and work samples together. If you can send them to the family members before the telephone conference, then all of you can discuss what has been accomplished by the child with the same point of reference. Finding creative ways to meet with families will give them the message that they are cared about and valued. The bottom line is that if families are not showing up for the conferences, it becomes your responsibility to pursue them and find a way to be successful.

It is preferable that most conferences last from thirty to forty-five minutes. Less time than that makes it difficult to review the observations and work samples in depth. However, some programs set up conference times so that parents first review the documentation without the educator. Parents arrive fifteen minutes before they meet with the teacher and spend that fifteen minutes looking through the observations, photos, and work samples and reading the summary report. Then the time spent conversing with the teacher can be about twenty minutes. An established agenda with time frames for each part will keep the conference on task and on time.

When you meet with families, good listening skills are of critical importance. By listening carefully, you will help family members feel validated and give them the message that their ideas are important and meaningful. It can sometimes be difficult to listen and really hear what family members are saying. Sometimes you are busy thinking about what you want to share regarding the child's growth and development. In that case you may not hear family members' concerns clearly. For example, your focus may be to talk about the child's development in all areas (cognitive, social/emotional, language, and physical). But the family may want to talk about the impact on their child of her grandmother's death. In such a situation it can be difficult to truly listen and respond to the family's concerns appropriately, especially within the time constraints of the conference. It might be necessary to schedule another time to get together to discuss their concerns. The time between these meetings can also provide you with an opportunity to reflect on their issues and be better prepared to discuss them. Being an effective listener does not mean that the family controls the conference or uses all of the time to discuss their issues, ideas, or concerns. It only means that you truly listen and respond to their thoughts in a way that lets them know that you appreciate and value their comments.

After you hear the family members' questions and concerns, the next part of the conference is spent going over the documentation that has been collected and formatted for the conference. When presenting documentation to the family, it is important to be prepared. If you want to talk about the child's growth in the area of math and science exploration, make sure that your documentation backs up your thoughts. Have pictures and work samples of the child engaged in math and science activities. If you want to suggest changes in an infant's feeding or sleep schedule, have several daily reports to support what you have been noticing about the child's patterns. Your concerns, if any, can come after you have shared some of the growth and development you have documented. It is much easier for families to hear your concerns when they have first seen examples of their children's progress. Teachers report that the documentation helps support their recommendations to families.

After you have shared the documentation and work samples you have compiled for the conference, you and the parents can set goals for the child for both the school and the home environments. This is a won-

> **Darlisa:** *Observation really helped us in dealing with parent conferences, where parents would always seem to be looking for the more traditional milestones for their child to be developing, ABC's, more academic or social. They'd say something like "I don't see my child interacting or having a lot of friends." But because we observed, we could look through the social/emotional development observations and say, "No, in this example, in writing down this observation, they do use their verbal skills in talking with other children."*

derful way for families to feel a part of the educational process of their child and to know that their contribution is valued by you and reflected in the goals of your program.

The last part of the conference is to let the families know how much you appreciate their coming and how important their input is to you in your planning. It is important to leave them with a convenient way to get in touch with you if they think of something else that they want to share. You also might want to follow up with a thank-you note for coming to reaffirm your commitment to them and to their children.

The rewards of a successful family meeting are great. When you use observational assessments as the format, family members are much more easily engaged and see more clearly just what their child is doing. They are also more aware of what you do with their child and how well you know him. Common ground is more easily reached through the use of an authentic representation of the child's growth and learning.

Peggy: *Having the documentation for family members to look at took pressure off of them. Parents are usually nervous and scared to hear what I am going to tell them about their child. And to sit down with a portfolio filled with my observations shows them that I am a professional and gives us a direction to go. It gives all of us a way to think about and plan for the next steps for the child. One mother came to the conference and then took the portfolio home to share with the dad. Later, she told me that when he looked at it, he got tears in his eyes. I think it is because he could tell, even without being there, that I know his child well and care about her.*

Observation Practice:
Observing for Developmental Capabilities

Purpose: To identify early literacy capabilities

What to Do: If you have access to the *Focused Observations* video, watch Vignette 9, "Listening to a Story," which shows Christian (2 yrs. 7 mos.). If you do not have the *Focused Observations* video, watch a child you know being read to by an adult.

As you watch the child, try to identify his interest in the story. Your observation notes should answer the following questions: Does he look at the pictures? Does he follow the story line? Does he verbalize in relation to the story? Does he stay until the story is finished? Remember to be factual and descriptive, not interpretive. Be prepared to share your experience with others.

Group Discussion: Share some of the anecdotes from the group. Look at the similarities and differences in the documentation from the group. Did people identify different capabilities? Why do you think that is?

Observation Practice:
A Focused Observation on Problem Solving

Purpose: To identify a child's problem-solving capabilities and relate them back to a different developmental source of information

What to Do: If you have access to the *Focused Observations* video, watch Vignette 10, "Working with a Puzzle," which shows Sydney (4 yrs. 10 mos.) and Jaiden (5 yrs. 1 mo.). If you do not have access to the *Focused Observations* video, watch a child you know putting a puzzle together.

Watch Sydney and Jaiden or the child you know, paying close attention to Sydney's or the child's problem-solving capabilities. Remember to be factual and descriptive, not interpretive, in your observation notes. After writing the documentation, look at a developmental source of information to identify problem-solving skills. Were you able to see a variety of problem-solving skills as the child worked to put the puzzle together? Be prepared to share your experience with others.

Group Discussion: Share some of the anecdotes from the group and the placement of the child's capabilities on the developmental checklists. Look at the similarities and differences in the documentation from the group. Did people identify different capabilities? Why do you think that is?

Observation Practice: Using Observation Information to Plan a Family Conference

Purpose: To practice preparing for a family conference using observational documentation

What to Do: Watch any vignette from the *Focused Observations* video or watch a child you know, and note what the child you know or the child in the video does and says. Remember to be factual and descriptive, not interpretive. Review your documentation, and decide what information you would want to point out to the family. Be prepared to share your experience with others.

Group Discussion: Share some of the anecdotes from the group as well as their thoughts about what to share in a family conference. Discuss how this information would be shared. Exactly what would you say? How would you anticipate the family members might react? You may even wish to role-play some of these discussions.

Reflection

Purpose: To reflect on what you know about developmental resources for assessment and effective strategies for family conferences.

What to Do: Think about the advantages and disadvantages of developmental sources of information that you have used or are familiar with. What sources of developmental information are you the most familiar with? What new ways of documenting children's developmental capabilities would you like to explore?

Identify potential barriers that may get in the way of early educators' implementing effective family conferences. How would you overcome those barriers?

Consider a teacher/family conference from the family's perspective. What are their fears and worries? What strategies can you use to address those fears?

Finding Your Observation Style

Purpose: To consider what developmental resources work best for your unique observation style and to learn from your experiences with family conferences how to make future conferences more successful.

What to Do: Respond to these questions in your journal:
- Which sources of developmental information best represent your understanding of child development? Why?
- Reflect on your own experiences with family conferences as a child, a student, a parent, and/or as an early educator. What have you found successful? What's been challenging? How could you overcome some of these challenges?

References

- Bagnato, Stephen J., John T. Neisworth, and Susan M. Munson. 1997. *Linking assessment and early intervention: An authentic curriculum-based approach.* Baltimore: Brookes.

- Berk, Laura E., and Adam Winsler. 1995. *Scaffolding children's learning: Vygotsky and early childhood education.* Washington, D.C.: National Association for the Education of Young Children.

- Bredekamp, Sue, and Carol Copple, editors. 1997. *Developmentally appropriate practice in early childhood.* Revised edition. Washington, D.C.: National Association for the Education of Young Children.

- Bricker, Diane. 1997. *Assessment, evaluation, and programming system (AEPS) for infants and children.* Baltimore: Brookes.

- Council for Chief State School Officers Early Childhood Education Assessment Panel. 2003. The words we use: A glossary of terms for early childhood education standards and assessment. http://www.ccsso.org.

- Dodge, Diane Trister, Laura Colker, and Cate Heroman. 2002. *The creative curriculum for preschool.* 4th edition. Washington, D.C.: Teaching Strategies.

- Erikson, Erik. 1963. *Childhood and society.* 2nd edition. New York: Norton.

- Gronlund, Gaye, and Bev Engel. 2001. *Focused portfolios: A complete assessment for the young child.* St. Paul: Redleaf.

- High/Scope Educational Research Foundation. 1992. *High/Scope child observation record for ages 2-6.* Ypsilanti, Mich.: High/Scope.

- Klein, Tovah P., Daniele Wirth, and Keri Linas. May 2003. *Play: Children's context for development.* Young Children.

- Kohn, Alfie. 2000. *The case against standardized testing.* Portsmouth, N.H.: Heinemann.

- Labinowicz, Ed. 1980. *The Piaget primer: Thinking, learning, teaching.* Menlo Park, Calif.: Addison-Wesley.

- Marsden, Dorothea B., Samuel J. Meisels, Judy R. Jablon, and Margo L. Dichtelmiller. 1994. *The work sampling system developmental guidelines.* 3rd edition. Ann Arbor, Mich.: Rebus Planning Associates.

- Marzano, Robert J., and John S. Kendall. 1996. *A comprehensive guide to designing standards-based districts, schools, and classrooms.* Aurora, Colo.: Mid-Continent Regional Educational Laboratory.

- Meisels, Samuel J., Dorothea B. Marsden, Amy Laura Dombro, Donna R. Weston, and Abigail M. Jewkes. 2003. *The ounce scale.* Lebanon, Ind.: Pearson Early Learning.

- National Association for the Education of Young Children (NAEYC) and National Association of Early Childhood Specialists in State Departments of Education (NAECS/SDE). 2003. Early childhood curriculum, assessment, and program evaluation: Building an effective accountable system in programs for children birth through age 8. http://www.naeyc.org.

- Wiggins, Grant P. "Assessment, Authenticity, Context, and Validity." *Phi Delta Kappan,* November 1993, 200–214.

chapter 5

Preschool Cho

Date Feb. 10

(may be used to tally one child's choi

Child(ren)

Art

Social/Emot

11 mins

nipulatives

mins.

0

How Do You Use Observation for Curriculum Planning?

You use observation to help you plan curriculum in two ways:

- right away, at the time of the observation

- over time, after you have observed multiple times

Sometimes you see a child doing something, and you immediately offer him your assistance. That's curriculum planning! It happens immediately. You make a judgment about what you are seeing, and you act on it.

At other times you watch the child more than once so that you can build a case about her capabilities and where she is having trouble. You might be trying to figure out her specific skills so that you can plan activities that challenge her at just the right level. You might be noticing that she is particularly interested in something. Or you might be wondering about her general personality and noticing that she has some times of the day when she copes more successfully than others. You observe her on different days and in different situations. That way you can understand her better and decide on a course of action that matches her needs more closely. This is also curriculum planning. It happens over time.

In the preceding instances, you are using observation to help you plan curriculum for individual children. You may focus your observations on one child in such a way that you can learn more about the following:

■ her developmental skills and capabilities

■ her behavior and ways she deals with frustration throughout the day

■ her choices and interests

■ her expression of her cultural background

You also use observation to plan for the whole group of children with whom you work. Again, you may act on what you see immediately, or you may observe the group over time before deciding what to do. When you are observing the whole group of children, your focus is broader. You may pay attention to the following:

■ how the room environment and materials are being used by the children

■ the success of activities that you have planned

■ what topics and activities children are particularly interested in

■ how the daily routine is flowing

■ where and when behavior problems are arising

■ how the cultural backgrounds of the children are being reflected in your activities and environment

Whether you are observing and acting immediately or doing so over time, the process of planning curriculum based on observation is cyclical and ongoing. First you observe. As you observe, you ask yourself questions. If you are watching a specific child, you may ask, "What can I do to help him?" If you are watching the whole group, you may ask, "What is working? What is not?" Then you make and implement a plan in answer to your question. And guess what: you observe again to see how well your plan works! The cycle repeats itself again and again.

The Assessment & Curriculum Process

1
Observe and document what you see
(evaluate your plan)

2
For an individual child:
Ask "What can I do to help this child?"
For the whole group:
Ask "What is working? What is not?"

3
Formulate a plan

4
Implement the plan

What Is Curriculum for Young Children?

It is very hard to define curriculum for young children because it can encompass everything that happens throughout the day. Curriculum is about children learning, whether it is alphabet letters, how to trust another person, or how to stack blocks so that they don't fall. Good curriculum will build on, sustain, and deepen children's interests in the world around them. And more long-lasting learning will occur when the curriculum is relevant and meaningful to children. In order to find out what is relevant and meaningful to them, you have to observe them in action!

Curriculum for young children is not oriented around textbooks, nor is it centered on teachers' imparting knowledge to the children. It is not limited to a theme or letter of the week. Curriculum is based on what works best with infants, toddlers, and preschoolers. It is appropriate for the ages of the children and recognizes individual differences as well. Good curriculum reflects the developmental needs and learning styles of young children and offers them these opportunities:

- hands-on exploration in a safe and carefully planned learning environment
- active involvement with materials that are just right for the age group
- lots of social interaction among children and adults
- opportunities for pretend play
- extensive exposure to books and music
- development of vocabulary through conversation
- strong, loving relationships among teachers and children, developing trust so that learning and risk taking can occur (Bredekamp and Copple 1997)

Many curriculum models and approaches are available to early educators. Some are tied to developmental checklists or criteria (*High/Scope; the Assessment, Evaluation, and Programming System [AEPS]*). Some advocate a more environmentally based approach, in which children explore within a carefully designed and organized set of learning areas and activities (the *Creative Curriculum*). Some emphasize following the children's lead so that curriculum emerges from the children's interests (emergent curriculum, the Project Approach, Reggio-inspired approaches). Many early childhood programs use a combination of these with adaptations to meet the social and cultural needs of the children and families they serve. Some program staffs write their own curriculum. For example, the Blackfeet Tribe in western Montana wrote a curriculum for its program based on language immersion in its native language. *Focused Early Learning: A Planning Framework for Teaching Young Children* (Gronlund 2003) provides a planning and reflection framework for integrating different approaches. All of these frameworks include several formal strategies for making individual adjustments to curricular planning and being responsive to children's interests as they develop. NAEYC does not endorse any one curricular approach, but it does provide frameworks and recommendations in order to evaluate the appropriateness of a curriculum. *Developmentally Appropriate Practice in Early Childhood Programs* (1997) devotes many pages to comparing inappropriate and appropriate curricular strategies.

Teaching looks different when you work with young children from what it looks like when you work with older ones. Teachers of young children provide nurturing and stimulation instead of lecturing or extensive paper and pencil tasks. If you work with infants and toddlers, you spend much of your time building a trusting, loving relationship with them, talking and singing with them, providing interesting and safe materials for them, and engaging in the everyday routines of feeding, diapering, and napping. If you work with preschoolers, you carefully arrange the environment so that they can explore materials, play with other children, and try out new things safely. You are there to guide and support them more than to tell them what to do.

You watch and interact with children as they play, go about their daily routines, and participate in teacher-designed activities because these are the ways they show you what they are learning and what they can and can't do. As you do so, you are learning about individual children and drawing conclusions about the whole group. And as you observe, you make decisions about what to do next.

Planning for Individual Children

If you are focusing on an individual child, you may decide to take a more passive role and let the child take the initiative. It's as if you and the child are dance partners and you are following the child's lead in the dance steps. At other times, you may take the lead, recognizing that you need to be more proactive to help the child. Sometimes it's best to stand back, watch, and encourage. At other times, it's more helpful to support the child with your assistance, to provide a scaffold that helps him do things that he cannot quite do on his own. And sometimes it's necessary for you to direct or demonstrate for the child so that he knows exactly how to go about something. You move back and forth between being more and less involved with the child. And as you figure out how extensive your involvement will be, you have several choices of what to do:

- you can observe and encourage her to continue what she's doing
- you can select different materials or change the environment in some way
- you can plan for specific teacher guidance and intervention
- you can use peer interactions
- you can design special activities
- you can bring in additional resources

The only way to judge the success of your planning is to try it out and observe to see what happens. Certain choices may be more effective when you are focusing on the child's developmental skills or behavior. Others may be more appropriate for helping you build on her interests or respond to her expression of her cultural background. And you can apply them while she is playing, engaged in daily routines, or joining in an activity that you have designed especially for her. Here are several examples of ways that early educators planned for individual children. You will see that their strategies working with each child varied based on the situation and the needs of the child.

In the following situation Kaylee's teachers observed and saw no need to intervene in any way.

> Kaylee (4 yrs. 5 mos.)
> After waking up from a nap, Kaylee walks to Riley and says, "Hey, Riley, come over here. I'm the teacher. You sit there and pay attention!" Then Riley says, "No, I don't want to play. I'm busy right now, okay?" Then Kaylee says, "Come on, Riley. Please. I'll play with you later. But you got to say the colors in English and Spanish. Come on. It won't take long. Okay, please?" So Riley says, "Okay. Red, yellow, orange, purple, white." Then Kaylee says, "Now, say it in Spanish!" Then Riley says, "White, blanco." They continue to play until it is time for snack.

Kaylee used language to engage Riley in play and was successful in negotiating with him to stay involved with her until snack time. Her teachers noted her high level of verbal interaction, interest in Spanish words, pretend play abilities, and social skills.

There are times when children need nothing more than your encouragement. Laughing along with a joyous child, sitting next to a child busy at work, quietly watching a child building with blocks, or verbally describing a child's problem solving with the waterwheel at the sensori-motor table are all ways of encouraging the child. Through your behavior you are saying, "I like what you are doing. Keep it up!" And through comments like "You are working hard on that painting," "I think you used every Lego in the bin," and "You can do it," you are expressing your acceptance of what he is doing and your expectation that he should continue in the direction he is going. In the following example, Robert, an infant, shows what he can do to solve the problem of getting a toy that he wants. Observing him and smiling as he succeeds are all the curriculum planning that may be necessary.

> Robert (10 mos.)
Robert crawls over to the shelf where the musical toys are kept. He pulls himself up to stand in front of the shelf holding the toy drum. He stands for a minute looking at the drum. Then he reaches for the drumstick attached to the drum. Using the drumstick, he pulls the drum toward him until he pulls the drum off of the shelf. He sits down on the floor and begins playing with the drum.

At other times when children are involved in an activity, you recognize that they could take this activity a bit further if they had some different materials. Your goal may be to lengthen their attention span and engagement. Or you may recognize that the skills they are demonstrating are ones that are easy for them. Therefore you want to extend the activity so that each child can use more complex approaches to the task or deepen his understanding of the concepts involved. You also may be building on an interest the child is showing in using particular materials. You want to provide additional opportunities for her to continue to follow up on that interest. The following anecdote describes just such a situation.

> Hudson (3 yrs.)
One day, Hudson went over to the block area and spent approximately ten minutes sorting through all of the unit block shapes. He then made a tower with five cylinder-shaped blocks. "Look what I did!" he called out to me. My co-teacher and I recognized that he was grouping objects and decided to provide additional materials for sorting and grouping to Hudson. Over the next few days, we provided him with colored plastic teddy bears in a large red basket. He got several small boxes off the shelf and sorted the bears by color so that red bears were together, yellow bears were together, and so on. He put both blue and purple into the same small box. On another day, he took small colored pegs and lined them up across the floor in a recurring pattern.

What other materials might you provide for Hudson to continue and extend his interest in sorting and patterning?

Dealing with difficult behaviors can be a very challenging part of your work with children. Sometimes you see a child take the same actions again and again with very poor results. You may feel that you need to be on constant alert as to that child's whereabouts. You may have to take steps to protect other children and remove the child from that area of the classroom. You may get to the point where you have to admit that you just don't understand the meaning of the child's behavior. As you read the following description, think about how taking the time to observe the situation helped the teacher see Jeremy's behavior more clearly and offer her assistance to him so that he could more successfully join in play.

> Jeremy (4 yrs. 3 mos.)
> I observed Jeremy closely over several days in the block area. Each day he would watch the children for a few minutes, especially two boys building complex block structures. Then, with no warning, he would wander over to where they were and knock down their structure.

After observing and documenting this for a few days, Jeremy's teacher began to realize that Jeremy lacked the social skills to enter into play with others. So she asked him if he wanted her to play with him. He immediately responded with an emphatic yes. From that point on, the teacher worked with him to help him learn appropriate ways to enter into play. As they played, the other boys came and joined them. The teacher modeled appropriate ways for Jeremy to play with them. After a few days she was able to sit close by but not be very involved. After a couple of weeks, Jeremy and his friends were playing cooperatively without any help from the teacher. A month or so later, he routinely asked other children if he could play with them or asked an adult for help. The teacher said, "If I hadn't taken the time to watch and wonder, and had assumed that Jeremy was misbehaving once again, I imagine that the outcome would have been very different for Jeremy."

Jeremy's teacher offered him the support he needed to help him move to the next level in his social skills. This process is called "scaffolding" and is based on the theories of Lev Vygotsky. As we discussed in Chapter 4, it involves providing just the right amount of challenge. You'll know it's just right because the child will be successful and begins to take responsibility for the task as his skill increases. This place where children do not quite have independent skills, but where they can be successful with adult or peer support, is called the zone of proximal development, or ZPD. When a task is within a child's ZPD, the child can become more and more independent in completing it.

> *According to Vygotsky, the role of education is to provide children with experiences that are in their ZPDs—activities that challenge children but can be accomplished with sensitive adult guidance. Consequently, adults carry much responsibility for making sure that children's learning is maximized by actively leading them along the developmental pathway. The teacher's role, rather than instructing children in what they are ready for or giving them tasks for which they have already acquired the necessary mental operations, is to keep tasks in children's ZPDs, or slightly above their level of independent functioning. (Berk and Winsler 1995, 26)*

Here is a description of a situation in which the adults determined that the best curricular strategy was to provide challenge for the child but also to offer adult help so that he could be successful and overcome his fear.

> ### Kyle (2 yrs. 2 mos.)
> Lately, when we go outdoors, Kyle spends time watching the other children climbing up and sliding down on the toddler-sized slide. We have asked him if he wants to go up. He shakes his head no and continues to stand nearby each day, watching the others. Even though he is saying no, we thought he was capable of climbing and sliding. Today I said to him, "Even though I hear you saying no, I think you really want to go up the stairs and down the slide. How about if I hold your hand and help you walk up and help you slide down?" He looked at me wide-eyed, took my hand, and off we went. After holding my hand tightly two times, he climbed up by himself with me standing close by.

Sometimes the best way to bring about successful results with a child is to use peer interactions. This can be an effective curricular strategy that can distract an angry child or bring out a more quiet one. In the following example the adults had observed Olivia over time, noticing her social isolation. They decided to use peer interactions as the way to move Olivia into more conversation and socialization.

> ### Olivia (4 yrs. 10 mos.)
> Usually Olivia plays and works all by herself. She does not seek out other children. If others sit down next to her, she will continue to work on her own, without much interaction. We have wanted to see if we could help

Olivia start engaging in more conversation and social interaction. So today, when she chose to go to the playdough table where dinosaur figures were also available, we suggested to Lydia that she join Olivia. Lydia is a very verbal and interactive child. We thought maybe the pairing of the two might bring Olivia out a little more. As they worked with the playdough and dinosaurs, both girls talked to each other about what the dinosaurs could do and eat. They then sat next to each other at snack time and talked as well! Our strategy was a success!

Sometimes your plan involves designing special activities or bringing in additional resources. Here is an example in which the adults recognized that they needed to have more resources in a child's first language to reflect his culture in the program and help develop his communication skills.

> **Yuta (2 yrs. 0 mos.)**
When Yuta began our program, he communicated through gesture only. We asked Mom to teach us some Japanese words, and we got a book with Japanese words in it. We also purchased a CD with Japanese music on it. Now Yuta responds to us in Japanese and does understand some English. He chooses the book frequently, bringing it to us to read to him.

And here is an example in which the adult provided additional materials, resources, and activities in response to a child's interest.

> **Taneisha (5 yrs. 2 mos.)**
After a heavy rainfall the sidewalk to the classroom was covered with earthworms. I took a cafeteria tray, went outside, collected several worms on the tray, and brought it inside for the children to study. All of the children were interested, but Taneisha more than anyone else. She spent fifteen to twenty minutes sitting quietly, watching the worms wriggle about on the tray. I asked Taneisha if she wanted to make worms out of playdough. Her eyes lit up. She played with the playdough near the tray of worms and made many different versions of her own earthworms. The next day I brought in books about earthworms. Taneisha spent much time looking at them and studying the pictures. I read several to her and invited her to make her own earthworm book. She dictated to me, "Some worms are long. They don't like the wet grass. They don't look like they have any eyes." Even though we put the worms back outside at the end of that rainy day, Taneisha stayed interested in the topic for several days afterward.

Planning for the Whole Group of Children

You also use observation to plan for the whole group of children with whom you work. When you do this, you are still watching individual children and noting what you are learning about them. But you are compiling this knowledge to use for different purposes. You are answering the question "What is working for this group of children? What is not working?" Then, based on the answers you are gaining to these questions, you may do some or all of the following:

- rearrange the room and change materials as needed, paying attention to children's choices and where behavior problems arise
- plan activities that will better engage the children
- plan based on children's interests and issues
- stay flexible within the daily schedule based on the needs of the children
- reflect children's cultural backgrounds and become more sensitive to their families' approaches to child rearing

When you are thinking broadly about curriculum for all of the children, your observations can help you understand more clearly where the children are coming from and help you make adaptations and changes so that you and the children feel successful.

Room Environment and Materials

You already observe intuitively every day to determine if the physical environment of your room is meeting the needs of the children. When you see poor behavior, misuse of materials, and high levels of frustration on the part of the children, you know that you are seeing warning signs that something is amiss. Loud noisy play rather than a pleasant hum of activity can be a sign that an area is not working well. Sometimes children totally avoid an area or set of materials. Sometimes too many children want to engage with a few specific items or in a space that is too small to accommodate them.

Many early childhood classrooms are organized into interest areas or learning centers. Older toddlers and preschoolers are given at least one fairly long block of time each day during which they can move from center to center, choosing from the variety of activities available and interacting with different children and adults. Most programs include the following interest areas:

- Art
- Blocks

Peggy: *I think that observation and documentation is the only way to ensure that I am doing what I want to do for and with children. When I want to make sure that each child is being given opportunities to learn at his own rate, I use observation and documentation to see if the children are reaching the goal or working toward it. I always make sure that I am following the children's agenda, meeting individual children's needs.*

- Dramatic Play
- Manipulatives
- Science/Math
- Movement/Music

Monitoring the children's choices in these areas, as well as their levels of engagement and interactions, can be a useful way to approach evaluating your environment. Some teachers use a check sheet like the following, where they can either record by tally marks the number of children who visit the area or list the children's names as they work and play there. We have provided two Choice Record formats in Appendix A that are ready to copy—one for preschoolers and one for toddlers.

You learn a lot about children by the choices of activities they make and the areas of the room they choose to spend time in. Often children choose to do something again and again. Their behavior may look repetitive to you. Yet there may be a very good reason why they are involved in the same activity or choosing the same materials.

- They may feel comfortable with that activity because it is familiar to them. They may have done it at home.
- They may be afraid to try something new.
- It may make them feel successful if they are able to do it easily. It's something they have accomplished.
- It may require them to use a skill that they are working on. In this case, they have almost mastered it and are practicing it again and again to get better at it.

When children choose areas of the room as their favorites, they are showing us more about their personalities and strengths. An artistic child may choose to paint and draw every day. At daily outdoor time, a

> **Robin:** *I am in a class-room with three-year-olds. Observing with more focus forces me to set the environment up in a way that's more process-oriented, so that it allows me the time to concentrate on the children and to observe them and be able to write down the things that I need to write down.*

Preschool Choice Record

(may be used to tally one child's choices or a group of children's choices)

Date _____   Child(ren) _____

Art	Social/Emotional	Dramatic Play
Manipulatives	**Science/Math**	**Music/Movement**
Library	**Sensory Table**	**Writing Center**

©2005 Gaye Gronlund and Marlyn James. May be reproduced for use by teachers.

Toddler Choice Record

(may be used to tally one child's choices or a group of children's choices)

Date _____   Child(ren) _____

Paint Easel	Blocks	Play House
Manipulatives	**Crawling Area**	**Climbing Structure**
Book Corner	**Sensory Table**	**Rocking Chair**

©2005 Gaye Gronlund and Marlyn James. May be reproduced for use by teachers.

very physical toddler may climb up to the top of the climber as she uses her big muscles to their fullest. A very verbal child may love to get other children to join him in pretending with dress-up clothes and dolls. He takes the lead, providing the script ideas and assigning roles because of his ability to use language effectively. Children may also avoid areas and activities that require skills they haven't developed yet. For example, children with poor fine motor skills may seldom choose to draw, write, or use scissors.

When observing children, you can use a Choice Record as a quick way to jot down information about their engagement in the areas of your room. As you watch the children, you note the areas they visit during a set period of time. If one child is being observed, a tally mark in various areas may be all that you record. You can also include the amount of time she stays engaged with the materials in that area. If you are observing several children, you can write their names in the areas that they visit that day.

Choice Records not only help you identify children's choices and interests but also can help you determine how effectively the environment is being used by the children. If you have lots of marks in one area and very few in another, you may want to make changes in the less popular one. Here are two examples of Choice Records—the first for a preschool child, including time tallies, and the second for a group of toddlers.

You can also pay attention to children's behavior and try to figure out where in the room you see problems develop. Keeping a record of where you see tears or hear angry words will help you rethink the arrangement of furniture, shelves, and materials. Making changes to

Preschool Choice Record

(may be used to tally one child's choices or a group of children's choices)

Date _Feb. 10_____   Child(ren) __Miguel___ 3 yrs. 8 mos._____

Art	Social/Emotional	Dramatic Play
11 mins		5 mins.

Manipulatives	Science/Math	Music/Movement
9 mins.	0	0

Library	Sensory Table	
0	15 mins.	

Toddler Choice Record

(may be used to tally one child's choices or a group of children's choices)

Date _April 15_____   Child(ren) _Makenra 1 yr 6 mos; Jesse 1 yr. 10 mos; Hurriell 2 yrs 0 mos_____

Paint Easel	Blocks	Play House
H	M, J	M, H

Manipulatives	Crawling Area	Climbing Structure
J	H, M	J

Book Corner	Sensory Table	Rocking Chair
	M J H	M

the arrangement of furniture, the organization and availability of materials, or the use of space based on those observations can often create dramatic and positive changes in children's behavior.

The first step is to document where inappropriate behaviors are occurring. Some teachers use small sticky notes and post them on the wall above the areas (out of reach of the children) where problems are seen. Doing this over a few days or a week's time will help identify the areas that need to be addressed. Sometimes you notice that traffic patterns are the source of problems; for example, children are crossing through the block area in order to get to dramatic play and accidentally, but routinely, knocking down others' block structures. A simple rearrangement of the block shelves to protect the building area and reroute the traffic flow is all that may be needed. It may help to get down on your knees so that you can look at the environment from a child's viewpoint (sitting on a child-sized chair can give you a similar vantage point). Looking from this perspective can help you evaluate safety issues: Are the corners on the cupboards showing signs of splintering? Is there enough space to get around the legs of the art easel? It can also provide insight into how clearly defined and inviting areas of the classroom appear to the children. If children are avoiding an area, it may be because they cannot easily see the materials available there or because the area is not clearly defined by the arrangement of shelves and tables.

Planned Activities

How do you know that an activity you planned for the children is successful or not? What are the signs? Evaluating the success of your planning is something that you do spontaneously, at the time you are involved with the children, and in reflection, as you think about it at a later time. You know an activity is successful when you notice signs like these:

- the children's eyes are bright; they smile and show enthusiasm as they participate in the activity
- the children stay for a long period of time (anywhere from ten to thirty minutes depending on their age)
- they tell you they like what they are doing, saying things like "This is fun!" "I like playdough."
- they ask to do it again or talk about it at a later time
- you see very few behavior problems as children engage in the activity
- the children take the activity to more complex and deeper levels than you had originally planned, adding their own ideas, bringing new materials, or using the materials in different ways

In contrast, how do you know when an activity is *not* working, when it is *not* successful? Sometimes you see difficulties arise right on the spot, and trying to keep the group on task can become nearly impossible, as in this example:

> Circle Time

At circle time the teacher reads a book with lively pictures and short, repetitive text—just right for the sixteen three-year-olds seated on the rug. The teacher has an engaging story-reading style. Most of the children appear to be listening and looking at the pictures, but two are obviously not paying attention. The teacher stops reading and admonishes, "Nathan, sit up" and "Jonathan, put your shoes on." A page or two later, she stops again and says, "Holly, hands to yourself." The children all look at Holly and begin to comment on whom she is touching and why. As the teacher returns to the story, more children fidget and a few begin to play with the toys on the shelf behind them. Before she gets to the end of the story, the teachers says in an exasperated voice, "Okay, everybody, this is the time to listen, not to play with your friends or with toys." As she continues, most of the children have lost interest in the story. Circle time ends with a frustrated teacher and squirmy children. (Loomis and Wagner 2005, 94)

Young children are brutally honest in letting you know that what you are doing with them is not of interest to them! They show this mostly through their behavior. Following are some of the ways you know that an activity is not successful:

- the children look away or get distracted or their eyes glaze over
- they wiggle or get more physical than the activity calls for, so that they may lose control of their bodies, getting silly or being rougher in their actions
- if they are monitoring their own involvement, they stay involved for a very short time and quickly move on to something of more interest
- their general behavior deteriorates
- they act unenthusiastic (no bright eyes, no excitement) and ask questions such as "Do I have to?" or "When can I leave?"
- they tell you, "This is boring" or "I already know how to do this"

When you see these behaviors you need to make a change in what you are doing, and the sooner the better! For the preceding circle time example, the teacher could have stopped reading the story and said, "I can see we have the wiggles today and aren't ready to listen. Let's put the book away and look at it another time. We'll do some dancing instead." Then she could put on some favorite music and provide an opportunity for children to use their energy in a much more fun and engaging way. She also could have ended circle time early and taken them outside to achieve the same end.

Sometimes you design an activity that addresses specific skills. You plan to work with a small group of children and will document what you see them doing so that you can assess their progress on these skills. For example, you may plan to have your two- and three-year-olds work with you on matching colors. You design a matching game using wallpaper samples cut into squares. At play time you call children to your table and expect them to join you in this activity as you document their matching capabilities on your clipboard. Some children may come readily; others may be reluctant. Some may enthusiastically try the matching game; some may only stay for a minute. You will know how successful the activity is when you look over the responses of all of your children and ask yourself these questions:

- Were the children interested and engaged? How did I know that?
- How many children participated?
- Did the children seem to enjoy the activity?
- Did I learn what I needed to learn about their skills? (Loomis and Wagner 2005)

Implementing teacher-designed activities such as this one may be more successful if you think of a variety of ways that you can meet your goal of learning about the children's matching skills. In addition to your wallpaper matching game, you could also have small colored blocks and colored bowls or trays, strings and colored beads, markers, and colored paper. You could offer a selection of matching activities to the children to give them a choice of materials that better match their interests and what they like to do. This selection may very well keep them engaged for a longer period of time and give you more information about how well they are recognizing similarities and differences across varying materials.

Children's Interests

Building on children's interests makes your curriculum more relevant to them. Sometimes children become absolutely fascinated with a topic such as dinosaurs or trains. They relate much of their play to this topic. They ask lots of questions and show excitement when you respond by providing materials and resources related to their interest. They engage more readily in activities and sometimes take their own level of exploration and knowledge deeper than you might have thought was possible. Think of how many young children have an extensive vocabulary of dinosaur names and traits and understand the basic definition of extinction.

Listening carefully to the questions children ask and paying attention to the play themes they are acting out help you identify their deep inter-

Peggy: *When I ask, "Is there something more you would like to learn about?" children usually produce a wealth of questions. For example, as part of our study of farms, children asked questions such as "Why is the milk always white even if the cows are different colors?" "Where do puppies come from, because my friend's dog had puppies?" and "I want to know about big fat pigs!" So one of our plans is to visit a farm and specifically try to learn more about their interests.*

ests and passions. You will also understand more about the knowledge they are constructing. You can pose your own provocations and ask open-ended questions to learn more about their thinking. One group of four- and five-year-olds showed interest in the pipes under the bathroom sink. One child asked, "Where does the water go?" The teacher responded, "Where do you think it goes?" This started an investigation for the group. They visited other bathroom and sink areas in the center. The teacher took notes on the number and size of the pipes. They flushed toilets and checked outdoor faucets and hypothesized about where the water went. The teacher brought in plastic pipes for building and tubes for using at the water table. She found books showing plumbing systems and underground sewer systems. She continually responded to the children's queries by asking for their thinking and by providing information and opportunities for them to figure things out for themselves.

Sometimes you see behavior that is silly and inappropriate because the children do not have information to explain what is happening. The fascination with each others' bodies and the sounds they make can easily turn into giggles or embarrassment and lead to misbehavior. You can provide books about human bodies and how the digestive system works to turn the silliness into understanding. Sometimes children behave in ways you do not understand. You see them acting out situations in your house corner that concern you. Or you see obsessive attention to play based on the latest movies and television shows. This play often deteriorates to the point where a child is hurt or angry. Here is a description of just such an incident:

> ## > The Doll Corner
> The four girls in the doll corner have announced who they are: Mother, Sister, Baby, Maid. . . . Charlotte is the mother because, she tells the others, she is wearing the silver shoes. . . .
>
> Karen: I'm hungry. Wa-a-ah!
>
> Charlotte: Lie down, baby.
>
> Karen: I'm a baby that sits up.
>
> Charlotte: First you lie down and sister covers you and then I make your cereal and then you sit up.
>
> Karen: Okay.
>
> Teddy watches the scene as he fills up the number board for the second time. Charlotte returns his stare and says, "You can be the father." He inserts the last two tiles and enters the doll corner.
>
> "Are you the father?" Charlotte asks.
>
> "Yes."
>
> "Put on the red tie."

She doesn't know Teddy's name yet, but she can tell him what to wear because she is the mother.

The girls look pleased. "I'll get it for you, honey," Janie says in a falsetto voice. She is the maid. "Now, don't that baby look pretty? This is your daddy, baby." Teddy begins to set the table, matching cups and saucers as deliberately as he did the tiles on the number board.

Abruptly, the mood changes. Andrew, Jonathan, Jeremy, and Paul rush in, fingers shooting. "We're robbers. Do you got any gold?"

"No," Charlotte says, stirring an empty pot.

Jeremy climbs on the refrigerator and knocks over several cartons of plastic food. "Put up your hands. You're going to jail!"

"We're telling!" The girls stomp out. (Paley 1984, 1–2)

Play that is influenced by the media can be very troublesome in early childhood programs. Problems arise because such play is imitative and is not as rewarding to children as play they have created from their own imaginations. Much intervention on your part may be necessary to protect children's safety and encourage more positive interactions. It's hard for you to want to build on the children's interest in this kind of play. Yet the underlying themes of feeling powerful and keeping safe are important and universal ones for children. "The sense of power and competence that is experienced in war play—as children pretend to be superheroes with super powers, for instance—can help children feel like strong and separate people who can take care of themselves" (Carlsson-Paige and Levin 1987). When observing children involved in play scripts that imitate Spider-Man movies or Power Rangers television shows, you can recognize the important developmental issues that children are exploring. If you only intervene and attempt to stop or forbid the play, you are missing the strong need that children have to feel powerful in a scary and violent world. You can recognize the play theme as an important one for children to explore and then intervene in ways to help the play move beyond mere imitation and develop instead into more complex and rewarding play. In this way you will help tame the inappropriate behaviors that arise and help children to take control of their play so that they feel empowered or gain a sense of resolution (Carlsson-Paige and Levin 1987).

Many early educators find that one way to encourage children to move beyond media-influenced play is to explore the same developmental themes of power, safety, and conflict resolution through children's literature about fairy tales, monsters, outer space creatures, dinosaurs, and scary things. In fact, much of children's fascination with dinosaurs probably comes from their deep, internal need for safety. They see dinosaurs as safe monsters because they are extinct.

In describing her attempts at working with children in their superhero play, Gronlund (1992, 24) wrote of her results, "The aggressiveness of the play lessened. As I watched more closely, I saw that most of the kicking and karate chopping was indeed an attempt at 'fake fighting.' . . . If play became overwhelming for a child, or if actions were leading towards out-of-control behaviors, I engaged the children again using the lingo of their play. . . . I began to realize that fairy tales provided an outlet for children to explore the very same themes that Ninja Turtles did. . . . Dinosaur parades; building the Troll's bridge for the staging of *The Three Billy Goats Gruff;* making monster masks; and doing many readings of [favorite monster books] . . . all became regular events in our classroom. My acceptance of the children's favorite shows allowed everyone to express their feelings more openly. . . . I, as a teacher, needed to recognize the ways boys and girls work through the issues of power, aggression, and violence as different, but interrelated, and help the children see the connectedness." For more information on working with children around issues of superhero and fantasy play in early childhood classrooms, see Eric Hoffman's book *Magic Capes, Amazing Powers* (Redleaf, 2004) and Diane Levin's book *Teaching Young Children in Violent Times: Building a Peaceable Classroom* (NAEYC, 2003).

Here are two examples of children playing out themes of power. As you read these, think about how you might interact with these boys in a way that respects the importance of the issues they are exploring and helps them keep the play productive and rewarding for them.

> **Wyatt (3 yrs. 6 mos.) and Salimu (3 yrs. 8 mos.)**
Salimu and Wyatt are playing in the sand table. They're putting sand into a container together. Wyatt says to Salimu, "Let's make a cake." Salimu replies, "Yeah, a bad cake." Wyatt then says, "Yeah, because we're bad guys." Wyatt says, "Bad guys making a bad cake." Salimu then says, "Yeah, with people on top. They got stuck in my mouth." Wyatt says, "Bad guy people are on top of the cake." Salimu says, "Real! We're gonna eat them."

> **Waylon (4 yrs. 8 mos.)**
Waylon is in the loft with four other boys playing firefighters. Waylon is in the front of the two other boys and says, "Let's go. There's a fire!" One boy moves forward, and Waylon tells him, "Get back, guys. Get back. You're supposed to be in the back. You're in the driver's seat." Then he yells, "Let's go! There's another fire!" He goes to the Artillier and pretends to spray the fire with a hose and yells again, "There's another fire!" They run back up

into the loft, and again Waylon looks to the front and tells one of the boys, "No, there's the driver's spot." Another boy tells him he is a Ninja Turtle, and Waylon says, "Ninja Turtles are not firefighters. This is a firefighter truck. Go find a Ninja Turtle truck."

Daily Routine

As you observe the children, you may find that certain times of the day go more smoothly than others. Focusing on how children negotiate time within the daily schedule helps you determine if there is an appropriate balance among activities, routines, and transitions throughout the day, varying passive and more active opportunities for children. Again, you tend to evaluate the flow of the routine intuitively each day. You recognize when children need a change in the pace of activities. However, observation can help you notice if one part of the routine is always problematic. Paying attention to that time of the day for a week or so can give you insight into the cause of the problem, so that you can address it in a thoughtful way. Making a change so that children are happily engaged is a smart decision.

Reflecting Children's Cultural Backgrounds

You can also focus your observations for curriculum planning on children's expression of their cultural backgrounds. This will help you notice if the curriculum is not matching a given child's or group of children's culture or family life. Then you can plan to reflect the child's heritage and family life in your environment, materials, and activities. You can include posters, books, ethnic baby dolls, and dramatic play items that represent cultures and peoples from around the world. You will be providing a window onto the cultures of the world and a mirror for the child's life experience that will make her feel welcome and validated, as the following story demonstrates.

> Visiting

Lucy, who was three years old, and her mother visited a new program to consider enrolling her. This program had posters of young children from around the world displayed at children's eye level, along with a variety of multicultural materials available to the children. As Lucy and her mother were led on a tour of the facility, Lucy noticed a contemporary picture of another Native child. She ran to the poster, pointed to the girl in the photograph, and with a big smile on her face said, "Oh, Mommy, look! She looks just like me." Lucy's mother later reported that this experience was a critical factor in her decision to enroll her child.

This story illustrates how much attention we must pay to ensuring that environments reflect all cultures. Early childhood programs throughout the United States reflect the diversity of the American population. Children and families with differing experiences, religions, languages, and values are expected to join together and form an accepting community, whether in the child care setting or the neighborhood. You can play an important role in helping integrate cultural differences while celebrating the unique characteristics of each family and individual. It's critical to move beyond artifacts, holidays, food preparation, and dress as reflections of culture, to incorporate values and beliefs that deeply affect children's everyday lives. It's only by doing so that teachers can provide culturally appropriate care for children.

Sometimes you see this expression of culture in the way a child goes about daily routines.

> ### Sleeping
A southeast Asian immigrant family enrolled their baby in an infant centerprogram. The baby had never slept by himself before, and when he was put into a crib off in a quiet, darkened room, he got very upset. It wasn't just the ordinary upset of a child who was resisting going to sleep even though tired; it was a panic reaction of a child who was very fearful of the situation. No matter what the staff tried to do to help this child sleep alone, nothing worked. He would sleep only near someone in the midst of the activity of the playroom. Being by himself to sleep was a fearful and foreign situation for him. (Gonzalez-Mena 1993, 30)

Views and values related to attachment and separation vary according to cultural expectations, beliefs, and life experiences. Some cultures stress autonomy and separateness, while others emphasize connection and dependence on others. Each family's behavior regarding separation and attachment looks very different based on the family's value system.

> ### Avi (3 yrs.)
Avi and his family had recently moved to the United States from Israel. Right away we noticed that Avi's mother was reluctant to leave him. She stayed for the entire three hours each day. As we thought about reasons for her reluctance, we imagined that a part of her hesitance was the fact that they had left a strife-torn country. We guessed that safety was probably an issue for this family. We wanted to give her and her son plenty of time to feel safe and to learn to trust us. So we just let her stay for the first three weeks of school. Then we asked her if she would be willing to go for a short walk each day. She agreed reluctantly and would always peek in the window before she would go for her walk to ensure that Avi was fine.

Slowly, she began to leave for longer and longer periods of time. After about the first two months of school, she felt comfortable leaving for the entire morning. Avi's mom became one of the most devoted parents we had and could always be depended on to help out in any way we needed. I often wonder how different this scenario might have been if we were not sensitive to the family's unique attachment and separation needs.

Some parents believe in holding their child more than others. Therefore, the child may expect more physical contact and holding from you. Separation is going to be a different process with each family. Being sensitive to these issues and asking the families about their beliefs, values, and life experiences will help you be more in tune with their children.

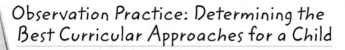

Observation Practice: Determining the Best Curricular Approaches for a Child

Purpose: To identify the best ways to support a child

What to Do: If you have access to the *Focused Observations* video, watch Vignette 11, "Working with a Puzzle," which shows Nate (3 yrs. 9 mos.). If you do not have access to the *Focused Observations* video, watch a child you know who is engaged in an activity that requires the support of a teacher.

Watch Nate or the child you know, and note what he does and says. Remember to be factual and descriptive, not interpretive. Identify in your notes when the child was most successfully engaged and when he had problems. How did the teacher's support help the child with the activity and with behavior? Identify ways you could help the child be successful in future interactions. Be prepared to share your experience with others.

Group Discussion: Share some of the anecdotes from the group, and discuss how the teacher's involvement helped the child's behavior.

Observation Practice: Encouraging and Extending a Child's Interests

Purpose: To determine ways to use materials to set up the environment and interact with a child to build on his interest

What to Do: If you have access to the *Focused Observations* video, watch Vignette 12, "Tubes and Bottles," which shows Elias (2 yrs. 1 mo.). If you do not have access to the *Focused Observations* video, watch a child you know as he plays.

Pay close attention to all of the things that Elias or the child you know is able to do and is interested in. Focus on how the environment is set up with materials that interest him and what the teacher does to encourage his interest and learning. Be prepared to share your experience with others.

Group Discussion: In what ways does the physical environment capture the child's interests? In what ways does the teacher encourage him as he explores the bottles and the tubes and watches what is happening outside? What might be some additional strategies to extend his interests and discoveries?

Reflection

Purpose: To reflect on how observation can assist curriculum planning

What to Do: Use these questions to plan individualized curriculum for children in your class.

1. Think of examples of when you have created a zone of proximal development (ZPD) for a child. Consider the following questions:
   > What was the specific activity?
   > How did you scaffold, or provide support, for the child to be successful? What were the results?

2. How do you ensure that children's interests are integrated into the curriculum?

3. How do you know that a curricular approach is culturally appropriate? What will you see as far as the environment, materials, and interactions?

Finding Your Observation Style

Purpose: To determine how your observation style relates to your planning of curriculum

What to Do: In your journal respond to these questions: What ways of planning for children do you tend to choose most often?

- through their play
- as they go about their daily routines
- in teacher-designed activities

Which do you find engage the children most fully? Why do you think that is? Make a commitment to try something new in your planning.

References

- Berk, Laura E., and Adam Winsler. 1995. *Scaffolding children's learning: Vygotsky and early childhood education.* Washington, D.C.: National Association for the Education of Young Children.

- Bredekamp, Sue, and Carol Copple, editors. 1997. *Developmentally appropriate practice in early childhood programs.* Revised edition. Washington, D.C.: National Association for the Education of Young Children.

- Carlsson-Paige, Nancy, and Diane Levin. 1987. *The war play dilemma: Balancing needs and values in the early childhood classroom.* New York: Teachers College.

- Gonzalez-Mena, Janet. 1993. *Multicultural issues in child care.* Mountain View, Calif.: Mayfield.

- Gronlund, Gaye. 1992. Coping with Ninja Turtle play in my kindergarten classroom. *Young Children* 1:21–25.

- Gronlund, Gaye. 2003. *Focused early learning: A planning framework for teaching young children.* St. Paul: Redleaf.

- Hoffman, Eric. 2004. *Magic capes, amazing powers: Transforming superhero play in the classroom.* St. Paul: Redleaf.

- Levin, Diane E. 2003. *Teaching young children in violent times: Building a peaceable classroom.* 2nd edition. Washington, D.C.: National Association for the Education of Young Children.

- Loomis, Catherine, and Jane Wagner. 2005. A different look at challenging behavior. *Young Children* 2: 94–99.

- Paley, Vivian Gussin. 1984. *Boys and girls: Superheroes in the doll corner.* Chicago: University of Chicago.

chapter 6

Preschool Cho

Date **Feb. 10**

(may be used to tally one child's cho

Child(ren)

Art		Social/Eme
11 mins		

nipulatives

mins.

0

How Do You Build a Case about a Child?

This chapter will give you the opportunity to pull together information about children in order to assess their development and plan curriculum that will best meet their needs. We will share several observation notes about preschoolers and toddlers so that you can practice evaluating each child's strengths and weaknesses and planning activities and teaching strategies for him. This is the all-important task of an early educator: reflecting on what you are learning about a child and figuring out what you are going to do for him.

When reviewing observation information you can ask yourself questions such as these:

- What can and does this child do? What are her interests, and how does she show them? What specific skills does she have?

- What would the next steps be for her in her development? What is she not doing yet?

- What would you plan to do with her to help her build on her strengths and interests or to work on what she is not doing yet? What materials, activities, teacher support, peer support, and special resources would you use?

We recognize the information you will be reviewing here is limited. You do not have the in-depth knowledge of these children that their teachers have. You do not know these children or work with them closely. However, we feel strongly that practice is important in becoming a better observer as well as in using the information gained through observation. We hope you will find the experience helpful in your learning process.

Claudia, A Four-Year-Old

The observation notes that follow document Claudia's development across several areas. All of these observations occurred over a three-month period in the fall. Read through these notes about Claudia and the reflection we did in answer to the questions we posed on the preceding page.

Claudia's Fall Language Observation

> (4 yrs. 1 mo.)
> Claudia announces, "I'm going to Tucson with my family—my mom and dad and my sister. And we are going to stay in a hotel with a swimming pool." She then carefully selects red, yellow, blue, and green markers and makes a rainbow. She then draws four people. She says, "Look. It's my family in a rainbow."

Claudia's Fall Problem-Solving Observation

> (4 yrs. 2 mos.)
> It is afternoon Discovery Time after naptime. The large pattern blocks are out on a table. The children have been exploring them the past two weeks. Claudia is at the table by herself. She takes a large yellow hexagon and adds six triangles. Then she starts to layer the shapes. She plays there for some time. Then her dad arrives to take her home. "Dada, come see what I'm doing," she says. She undoes her work and redoes it exactly the way it was.

Claudia's Fall Social/Emotional Observation

> (4 yrs. 2 mos.)
> Claudia has become more comfortable separating from her parents at drop-off time. Today she comforts Emilia, who cries after her mom leaves. Claudia says, "It's okay. Mommy's coming back." She looks at me and says, "Mommy always comes back, right, Michele?" I smile and nod yes. Claudia gently puts her arm around Emilia and says, "I miss my mom. But see. I'm not crying." At pickup time Claudia tells Emilia's mom, "Emilia was crying for you, but I told her you would come back."

Claudia's Fall Writing Observation

> (4 yrs. 1 mo.)
> Claudia often asks for the Sleeping Beauty story tape. She often acts out the story. Today she gets lined story paper and says, "I'm writing the Sleeping Beauty story." She then draws a picture with black pen and paints it with watercolors. "This is the picture of her sleeping on the bed." (see sample at right)

Claudia's Fall Gross Motor Observation

> (4 yrs. 2 mos.)
> Claudia plays on the climbing equipment with Quinn and Fernando. All three of them are growling and roaring. Claudia climbs easily up the ladder to the platform. Quinn says, "Okay, I'm a baby jaguar." He paws the air in front of Claudia. She responds by saying, "Now there are two baby jaguars!" She moves quickly around the platform, jumps on the slide, and slides down. Then she runs around and climbs back up again.

What Does Claudia Do?

Here are the questions to consider: What can and does this child do? What are her interests, and how does she show them? What specific skills does she have? Try to answer them for yourself before reading the next section.

Claudia uses language to talk about her family and life experiences and to communicate with others. She showed great complexity in her design with the blocks and was proud to show her dad what she could do and re-created the design exactly. She shows interest in pretend play and in writing. She makes letter-like shapes in her writing and is not yet making all letters correctly. She uses her body with balance and agility as she runs and climbs. She has an awareness of her emotions and the emotions of others and can respond with empathy.

Next Steps for Claudia

What would the next steps be for Claudia in her development? What is she not doing yet?

Claudia is showing success in all of the areas documented in these observations.

Next steps will involve helping her to continue to use language effectively, to provide opportunities for her to use her large muscles, to solve even more difficult problems, and to build on her interest in writing.

Planning for Claudia

What would you plan to do with her to help her build on her strengths and interests and to work on what she is not doing yet? What materials, activities, teacher support, peer support, and special resources would you use?

One strategy might be just to continue to encourage her conversational language usage, modeling back to her more complex language. Providing more complex materials for her to use for creating and representing her ideas would build on her problem-solving capabilities. Perhaps she would enjoy working with a set of gears or a marble run that requires planning in order to be successful. You could follow up on her interest in jaguars and other animals and bring in nonfiction books about them. Providing some cards with familiar words for her to copy, such as "I love you," might provide a scaffold to take her to the next level of writing skills. She could choose some of the words and phrases that she would like to have as models on the cards. You could also encourage her to continue to show empathy to other children and ask her to be Emilia's special helper at arrival time.

What other strategies do you think would work well to help Claudia continue to grow and develop in these areas?

Corey, A Toddler

The observation notes that follow document Corey's development in the fall and in the spring. These notes are paired together specifically to track his progress in several developmental areas. Read through these notes about Corey. Then add your own thoughts to the answers we gave to the reflection questions listed earlier.

Corey's Fall Language Observation

> (1 yr. 2 mos.)
> Corey was sitting in the block center playing with a bucket of blocks. The other teacher in our class walked in, and Corey looked up at her and said, "Hi." He also says, "Mama," "Dada," "kitty," "dat" (for that), and "ball."

Corey's Spring Language Observation

> (1 yr. 6 mos.)
> Corey chooses a book called <u>Can You Hop?</u> from the library center. He takes the book over to Ms. Dorothy, who is sitting in a rocking chair. He turns around so she can pick him up and says, "Up, pease." This is the first time he has said that. In the fall his vocabulary was limited, but now he points at everything and says, "Dat?" and sometimes repeats what he hears us tell him it is.

Corey's Fall Problem-Solving Observation

> (1 yr. 2 mos.)
> Corey sees another child playing with the stacking rings. He wants to play with the rings, too, so I get some for him. He removes the rings one at a time. He replaces them on the post in random order. He plays a little while longer, maybe three minutes. Then he is on the go again, crawling across the room toward the bookshelf.

Corey's Spring Problem-Solving Observation

> (1 yr. 7 mos.)
> Today Corey picks up the whole set of stacking rings and turns it upside down. All the rings come off. He then starts replacing them one by one in random order using his right hand. He picks it up and dumps all of the rings off again. He starts to put the rings back on with his right hand. Then he picks up a toy snake in that hand. Holding it, he finishes by putting the last ring on with his left hand. He is successful, but he does not have the rings stacked in any particular order.

Corey's Fall Social/Emotional Observation

> (1 yr. 1 mo.)
> When Corey arrives in the morning and sees me, he smiles broadly and laughs. Then he reaches for me to hold him. He pats me on the back and gives me kisses on my face.

Corey's Spring Social/Emotional Observation

> (1 yr. 5 mos.)
> I hold one of the children on my lap. She is not feeling well. Corey comes over and pats the child on her leg. Then he gives her a toy he has in his hand.

Corey's Fall Fine Motor Observation

> (1 yr. 3 mos.)

Corey comes to the table where he sees other kids coloring. He chooses a purple marker. He holds the marker in his right hand with his fingers. He makes a few random marks up and down and side to side. (see sample at left)

Corey's Spring Fine Motor Observation

> (1 yr. 8 mos.)

In the fall Corey used markers with little control. Now he uses great control to make random horizontal marks. He chose a blue marker and held it in his right hand, full fisted, upside down and made a few random marks back and forth. He then switched to his left hand, which he held full fisted upright for a few random strokes. He went back to his right hand and this time held it in his fingers like a pencil and made a few more horizontal strokes. He also pounded on his paper to make some dots and showed signs of attempting to make circles. (see sample below)

Corey's Fall Gross Motor Observation

> (1 yr. 2 mos.)

Corey is just beginning to walk without holding on to something or someone. He falls occasionally, but not often. Although his balance is steady, he still will crawl very fast much of the time. Today he walked away from the snack table toward the aquarium. He fell on his bottom and quickly crawled the rest of the way.

Corey's Spring Gross Motor Observation

> (1 yr. 7 mos.)

Corey hardly crawls at all anymore. He walks easily and even runs without falling. Today, outdoors, he becomes fascinated with the wood chips. He runs to the climber area, squats down, and picks up several wood chips in his hands. Then he throws them up in the air and laughs as they land all around him.

What Does Corey Do?

Try to answer these questions about Corey before reading further: What can and does this child do? What are his interests, and how does he show them? What specific skills does he have?

Corey is labeling objects in his environment and asking his teacher to name things for him. He is able to combine two words and ask his teacher to read to him, by getting a book and saying, "Up, pease." Corey is developing an understanding of cause and effect, taking the rings off and putting them back on. While he is not yet putting them back on in order, he does understand the concept of stacking the rings and puts all of the rings back on. Corey has formed a trusting and comfortable attachment with his teacher and separates easily from his family members. He is also aware of the feelings of others; you could see this as he tried to comfort another child with the toy. Corey is taking time to use different pens and pencils as he experiments with art. He has moved from making random marks on his paper to experimenting with a variety of marks, even trying to make circles on his paper. He is able to run and throw small objects.

What's Next for Corey?

Now answer these questions, again before you read further. What would the next steps be for him in his development? What is he not doing yet?

Corey's development in all of the above documented areas shows his success. The next steps might be to continue to support his growth and development by ensuring that he has ample opportunities to use language, to problem-solve, to use fine and gross motor skills, and to interact with the adults and the children in the environment.

Planning for Corey

Finally, use the information in the preceding observations to think about planning for Corey. What would you plan to do with him to help him build on his strengths and interests and to work on what he is not doing yet? What materials, activities, teacher support, peer support, and special resources would you use?

One strategy might be to make sure that there are new books with pictures of things that he can label and to continue to read to him and converse with him using short, simple sentences, encouraging his growth in sentence length. Another strategy might be to provide him with different cause-and-effect toys such as simple shape sorters. You could also give him containers of things that can be dumped out and put back in, such as a basket full of balls of various sizes. Something else to do might be to encourage his awareness of others by talking about how other children are feeling, labeling his feelings and the feelings of others as they occur. As Corey's interest in drawing continues to grow, it will be important to make sure that there are ample opportunities for him to do so. Continuing to offer him opportunities to walk, run, balance, climb, and throw will build on his growing gross motor skills.

What other strategies do you think would work well to help Corey continue to develop in these areas?

Here are observation records about two more children. Read through these observation records and practice pulling the information together and building a case about each child. Answer the questions we have posed, and consider any other possibilities for ways to assess both children's development and plan appropriate curriculum for them.

Glenda, A Two-Year-Old

This observation record contains spring observation notes only. How does the information affect your ability to understand this child?

Glenda's Spring Problem-Solving Observation

> (2 yrs. 7 mos.)
Glenda plays with blocks and says, "I make a chair for my baby." First she lines the blocks in a row. Then she stacks some on top of each other. They fall, and she picks them up and builds again. Finally, she tells her mom, "Look at the table and chair I make for my baby." She then takes the doll and sits her on the chair she made out of blocks.

Glenda's Spring Language Observation

> (2 yrs. 7 mos.)
During playgroup Glenda and I play with Mr. Potato Head. Glenda's friend comes into the room, and Glenda says, "Come and play," and "Come sit down." She also says, "Where does this go?"

Glenda's Spring Fine Motor Observation

> (2 yrs. 7 mos.)
During this home visit I offer Glenda pencils, colored markers, and a dry-erase marker. She chooses the dry-erase marker and board. She holds the marker with a three-fingered grasp. She draws several small circles with a line coming down and tells me she has made balloons.

Glenda's Spring Social/Emotional Observation

> **(2 yrs. 8 mos.)**
> During playgroup another child begins to cry for his mom, who is in the other room at the parent meeting. Glenda sees him crying and goes to the shelf. She gets a tissue from the tissue box and gives it to him. He grabs the tissue and wipes his tears. Glenda smiles and pats him on the back.

Glenda's Spring Gross Motor Observation

> **(2 yrs. 6 mos.)**
> At the home visit today Glenda and I go out in her backyard and play on the swing set. Glenda sits on the swing and asks me to push her. I do so, and she starts yelling, "No, not so high!" and begins to cry. I stop the swing and help her get off. Then I ask her if she wants to go on the slide. "No, I'm scared," she says. "I'll help you," I offer. "No, let's just swing a little bit." So she climbs back on the swing, and I push her very gently so that the swing moves only a little bit. She asks to go back inside after five minutes outdoors.

Reflect on the observations above and answer these questions:

■ What can and does this child do? What are her interests, and how does she show them? What specific skills does she have?

■ What would the next steps be for her in her development? What is she not doing yet?

■ What would you plan to do with her to help her build on her strengths and interests, or to work on what she is not doing yet? What materials, activities, teacher support, peer support, and special resources would you offer?

Niko, A Four-Year-Old

This observation record includes both fall and spring observations so you can note Niko's progress across time.

Niko's Fall Language Observation

> **(4 yrs. 6 mos.)**
> Niko is playing with some small toy people outside of the doll house. I ask him if he can do the following: "Can you open the house, put the baby in its bed, and then put the little boy on the potty?" He follows all of the instructions correctly, looks at me, and asks, "Now what?" We do another set of three directions, and he follows all of them correctly too. He says, "This is easy, Ms. Kathy! I can do this."

Niko's Spring Language Sample

> (4 yrs. 11 mos.)
Mateo and Niko build an "island" with the hollow blocks. Then, using a clipboard with paper and pencil, they take turns drawing the "map" to show where the island is located. Mateo tells Niko to jump off the island and go into the water. Niko asks, "Are there any fishes in here?" Mateo says, "You're a mommy, now." Niko replies, "No, I'm not. I'm a captain." As other children join in the play, Mateo announces, "We're pirates." "Aye, aye, matey," says Niko. The play ends up involving treasure (dress-up necklaces), food, and a measuring tape.

Niko's Fall Problem-Solving Observation

> (4 yrs. 7 mos.)
When Niko is playing with small manipulative figures, I encourage him to find all of the creatures that are the same shape. At first he focuses on the color. After I model finding different shapes, he sorts them by shape. Then he gets distracted and sorts by color. Donald points it out, and Niko moves his creatures to the correct shape bin.

Niko's Spring Problem-Solving Observation

> (4 yrs. 11 mos.)
Niko chooses games from the game center two or three times a week. His favorite is Candyland. Niko will often play by himself, moving the pieces randomly around the board or matching the color cards with spaces on the board. At the suggestion of a teacher, he will invite a friend to play with him and will play for five to ten minutes.

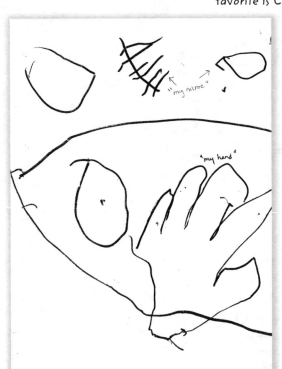

Niko's Fall Writing Observation

> (4 yrs. 8 mos.)
Niko chose to go to the Art Area today. He took a blue marker and paper to use. He sat at the art table looking at what other children were drawing on their papers. He traced his left hand and made some letter-like shapes at the top of his paper. "That's my name," he said. He used his right hand throughout, holding the marker with his thumb, pointer, and middle fingers. (see sample at left)

Niko's Spring Writing Observation

> (5 yrs. 1 mo.)

Niko often goes to the writing center now and writes on lined and unlined paper. Today he wrote chains of letters in a spiral notebook. When I asked him about his writing, he told me, "I wrote my mom's name, my aunt's name, my dad's name, and my brother's name." I labeled each as he pointed them out to me. He used his right hand, holding the marker correctly. (see sample at right)

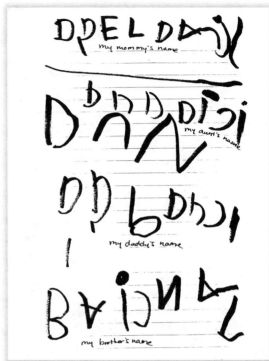

Niko's Fall Social/Emotional Observation

> (4 yrs. 7 mos.)

One of the activities that Niko often chooses outside is riding bikes. Today, when he got off his bike to go play somewhere else, another child jumped on his bike. When Niko returned and saw the child, he said, "Hey, that's my bike." The other child said, "No, it's mine." Niko walked over to him and pulled the handlebars on the bike, saying, "Get off. It's mine." I walked over and asked, "What's going on?" Niko said, "This is my bike." The other child said, "No, it's mine." I asked, "What do you think we should do?" Niko said, "I'm mad because he took my bike." "Where were you when he took your bike?" I asked. "Over there," he said, pointing to the sandbox. By this time the other child had lost interest in the bike, and Niko jumped back onto it and rode away.

Niko's Spring Social/Emotional Observation

> (5 yrs. 0 mos.)

Today, during outside play, Niko and another child were playing at the water table with small cars. Another child attempted to join in the play, bringing a car that was muddy. Niko said, "Don't bring that big car in here because it's dirty." The other child ignored him. Niko then grabbed at the car and said, "You are making the water all dirty. Look." They pulled the car back and forth for a few seconds, and then Niko let go. He grabbed another small car that was in the water and handed it to the child, saying, "Do you want to play with this one? It's clean." The child took the clean car and put the dirty one down to the side of the table. They continued to play together for another ten minutes.

Niko's Fall Gross Motor Observation

> (4 yrs. 8 mos.)

It is Niko's turn to crawl like an alligator during a large group activity. He is able to keep his tummy on the ground and pull himself around the classroom with his arms. He has a big smile on his face.

Niko's Spring Gross Motor Observation

> (5 yrs. 0 mos.)
I observed Niko walking around the swing area, balancing on the wooden planks that surround our playground. He concentrated on each step and did not fall once as he went around the whole area!

Reflect on the observations above and answer these questions:
- What can and does this child do? What are his interests, and how does he show them? What specific skills does he have?
- What would the next steps be for him in his development? What is he not doing yet?
- What would you plan to do with him to help him build on his strengths and interests and to work on what he is not doing yet? What materials, activities, teacher support, peer support, and special resources would you use?

Observation Practice: Building a Case about a Child

Purpose: To practice pulling together information about a child in order to assess his development and plan curriculum that will best meet his needs

What to Do: If you have access to the *Focused Observations* video, watch Vignette 13, "Making Music," Vignette 14, "Listening to a Story," and Vignette 15, "Playdough, Cups, and Binoculars," all of which show Christian (2 yrs. 7 mos.). If you do not have access to the *Focused Observations* video, watch a child you know during multiple activities across time.

Observe the child doing the activities, and take notes about the things the child does. Remember to be factual and descriptive, not interpretive. Then, using your notes, answer the following questions:

- What can and does this child do? What are his interests, and how does he show them? What specific skills does he have?
- What would the next steps be for him in his development? What is he not doing yet?
- What would you plan to do with him to help him build on his strengths and interests and to work on what he is not doing yet? What materials, activities, teacher support, peer support, and special resources would you use?

Reflect on your ideas about the child's accomplishments, interests, and needs and about the next steps you planned for him. Be prepared to share your experience with others.

Group Discussion: Share your ideas about the child's accomplishments, interests, and needs. Compare the next steps that you planned for him.

chapter 7

How Do You Continue to Grow as an Observer?

Throughout this book we have presented many ways for you to use observation and documentation to get to know children better. We hope that you will use what you learn by observing children to create opportunities for them that maximize their development.

We have encouraged you to take into account your personality style and the setting in which you work with young children. Doing so will help you become a more effective observer. Being prepared and ready for children to show you what they can do will help you to see much more. Trying out clipboards, sticky notes, and Quick Check Recording Sheets will help you to figure out your own documentation style. Having writing tools handy and several clipboards or documentation sheets available will help you capture documentation of children in action in a busy classroom. Recognizing your own ability to remember what happened so that you can write a clear description will determine when you write it down. If you tend to forget, you will write down observations as you see them, or as quickly as you can afterward. If your memory is good, you may be able to wait until a quieter moment in the day, such as naptime, to write down what you saw and heard.

Keeping in mind the purposes for your observations will help you be focused and clear on what needs to be documented and what you are going to do with the information. Are you observing an individual child in order to assess her development? Or are you observing to see how the group of children is using the room arrangement and materials to their fullest? Are you trying to find out if your curriculum plans match the needs of particular children? Or are you just trying to get more acquainted with the interests of the children in your program so that you can build on those interests? What you learn through observation can be used for both assessment and curriculum planning.

Developing your own ability to be open and ready to see children's growth and learning as they play and interact is an ongoing process. If you are new to the field of early education, you may not see children's capabilities as clearly as a more experienced teacher. Give yourself time to watch children and to learn to see development in action. Think of yourself as a researcher in the field of child development. Ask yourself, "What are the children showing me? What can each one do?" Writing only the facts, with no interpretations, will help you to collect evidence for your research. Relating that evidence to developmental checklists and resources will educate you in reasonable expectations for children at different ages.

Even experienced early educators can grow and learn as observers. Developing more awareness of the filters through which you see the world is an important first step in the process of growth. Sometimes such steps are difficult. Self-reflection and willingness to discuss issues of bias and prejudice with colleagues can improve your ability to record observations that are grounded in truth, rather than in preconceived notions or skewed views of children.

Adapting to Each Early Childhood Setting

Each early childhood setting is unique. You may work in a large child care center or a small preschool program. You may run your own family child care business or work in a Head Start program. You may do home visits regularly or be housed in a public school setting. No matter what your setting, you will need to figure out how to make observation work for you by creating a sustainable system.

Some of you work in teams. Dividing the tasks up among the members of your team ensures that all children will be observed and that documentation will include all areas of development. This requires communication among all of the staff involved. Setting aside time to discuss who will observe and when the observation will be written down is necessary. Having regular team meetings, even for five to ten minutes, will help everyone be on the same track and provide an opportunity to share what has been observed and what the next steps will be. This reflection and sharing are essential to tying observation to curriculum planning.

For those of you who work in family child care, or settings where you are alone with children, planning ways to fit in observation and documentation will be necessary. Recognizing that your primary role is to take good care of children will help prioritize your efforts. Yet always having writing tools available to write down what you see the children doing will help you be prepared for documentation. And setting aside reflection time for yourself will help you plan activities and strategies that are more in tune with the children in your care.

Whether you are just starting out or you have been using observation and documentation already, the following suggestions will help you create and maintain a system that will be successful.

- Create a learning environment conducive to ongoing observation.
- Begin and proceed gradually.
- Start with easy techniques.
- Stay organized and current.
- Enlist the aid of other people.
- Make observation a normal part of classroom living. (McAfee, Leong, and Bodrova 2004)

Throughout this book we have asked you to keep a journal in response to the activities and questions at the end of each chapter. Our goal was for you to find your unique style as an observer. We encourage you to continue to use your journal as you reflect on the process. This ongoing reflection will aid in your efforts to integrate observation into your daily routine. Journaling will enable you to think about the highs and lows of your implementation process and to brainstorm ideas and techniques for success. Change only comes with practice. And the best learning comes from solving the problems that arise from your trials and errors.

Being in the Moment with Children

Children honor us by allowing us to witness their ability to be truly who they are as they negotiate their environment and use their bodies and minds to learn about the world and the people in it. Early childhood is perhaps the only time in the life cycle, certainly during the whole period of childhood, in which children are open and uninhibited, playing and interacting freely. As early educators we are very fortunate to be able to watch this process. To be able to fully appreciate and enjoy the growth and learning of the children in our care, we need to reflect on what we see children doing and remember that at the heart of the matter is learning to be in the moment with each child.

Curtis and Carter (1996, 174–76) suggest several useful dispositions for early educators to acquire as part of their personal and professional development. These dispositions apply to professional development in observation as well.

- Delight in and be curious about children's development.
- Value children's play.
- Expect continuous change and challenge.
- Be willing to take risks and make mistakes.
- Provide time for regular reflection and self-examination.
- Seek collaboration and peer support.
- Be a professional watchdog and a whistle-blower.

The last disposition listed above has particular significance because the effective use of observation provides us with an opportunity to grow as advocates for children and as professionals in the field of early childhood. As we have seen, professional recommendations from throughout the field of education advocate for observational assessment rather than testing of young children. As early childhood professionals, we must take a stand on behalf of children and inform others of appropriate ways to assess young children's development. We can demonstrate the effectiveness of observational assessment that is grounded in objective documentation and tied to accepted and culturally sensitive developmental standards. By educating ourselves and joining together with our colleagues to speak up and share what we know about assessment, we can make a difference in children's lives.

In some settings you may not be able to choose your assessment tool or methodology. Many state and federally funded programs are mandated to use specific assessment systems. If you find yourself in such a situation, you can still try to do what is best for the children. Even though the mandated system may not be observational in nature, you can make observation and documentation an integral part of your practice. Keep watching the children. Keep taking anecdotal records. You know that you are gaining important information about the children and their development.

Watching Phoebe

For the final vignette in our accompanying video, we have chosen footage of a three-year-old girl running freely on a playground. She moves from a climber and slide to a balance beam to a set of swings. Throughout, she has a broad grin on her face, a sense of joy in her movements, and confidence in her own physical abilities. All of this takes place on a lovely spring day. Our purpose in choosing this particular vignette to end our video is to help early educators remember that at times the most important task in observing a child is to enjoy her. Phoebe does not need intervention or specific curricular planning. Yes, her physical capabilities could be assessed as a result of observing her actions. However, she appears to be deriving so much pleasure from her running, climbing, swinging, and balancing that doing a formal assessment of capabilities seems beside the point.

This is a perfect opportunity to return to the meaning of the word "assess." In Chapter 4 we noted that this word comes from the Latin verb "assidere," which means "to sit with." Enjoying children, being in the moment with them, and observing their actions for multiple purposes can truly be a form of sitting with them. Being the assessor, the one who sits beside, has the alternative meaning of "the one who shares another's rank or dignity" (Wiggins 1993 in Marzano and Kendall 1996, 123). When enjoying a child in action, each of us is given the opportunity to silently thank her for honoring us by sharing a small part of her life with us. Sit back. Smile. Rejoice with Phoebe, as you will with the children in your care, as she rejoices in her very being. Celebrate childhood. Be in the moment with children. And reflect on how you are learning and growing because you can observe children and learn from them.

Observation Practice: Celebrating a Child and Being in the Moment

Purpose: To learn to enjoy children's exuberance and zest for life

What to Do: If you have access to the *Focused Observations* video, watch Vignette 16, "Outdoors," which shows Phoebe (3 yrs. 0 mos.). If you do not have access to the *Focused Observations* video, observe a child as she plays outside, running, jumping, and climbing.

Observe the child without taking notes or worrying about observing for assessment or curricular planning. Instead, let yourself be with the child as she openly shares her enthusiasm and energy. Appreciate her as she enjoys the pleasures of being a child. Celebrate and enjoy what she does. Be prepared to share your experience with others.

Group Discussion: Share your feelings as you watched the child run, jump, and climb. Talk about the importance of being in the moment with children and having an appreciation for being a part of their enthusiasm and zest for life.

Reflection

Purpose: To reflect on your own growth and learning

What to Do: Continue to use your journal as a way to reflect on your own growth and learning as you observe the children in your care. Use your journal as a means of remembering the importance of observation for assessment and curriculum planning as well as for enjoying children and being in the moment with them. Continue to value how young children honor us by sharing their openness and honesty.

References

- Curtis, Deb, and Margie Carter. 1996. *Reflecting children's lives: A handbook for planning child-centered curriculum.* St. Paul: Redleaf.

- Marzano, Robert J., and John S. Kendall. 1996. *A comprehensive guide to designing standards-based districts, schools, and classrooms.* Aurora, Colo.: Mid-Continent Regional Educational Laboratory.

- McAfee, Oralie, Deborah J. Leong, and Elena Bodrova. 2004. *Basics of assessment.* Washington, D.C.: National Association for the Education of Young Children.

- Wiggins, Grant P. "Assessment, Authenticity, Context, and Validity." *Phi Delta Kappan,* November 1993, 200–214.

appendixes

Appendix A:
Forms and Formats

Teachers may reproduce the forms on the following pages for personal and classroom use only. These forms can also be found on the Redleaf Press Web site, www.redleafpress.org, by clicking on the title of this book.

Facts/Interpretation Form

Date _____   Child _____

Facts	Interpretation

Observation Record

Child's Name _____

Language	Social/Emotional

Physical (gross and fine motor)	Creative

Cognitive (math, problem-solving)	Early Literacy (reading & writing)

Quick Check Recording Sheet

Children's Names	Date & Activity	Date & Activity	Date & Activity	Date & Activity

Brief Notes Recording Sheet

Children's Names	Date & Activity

Preschool Choice Record

(may be used to tally one child's choices or a group of children's choices)

Date _____   Child(ren) _____

_____

Art	Social/Emotional	Dramatic Play

Manipulatives	Science/Math	Music/Movement

Library	Sensory Table	Writing Center

Toddler Choice Record

(may be used to tally one child's choices or a group of children's choices)

Date _____   Child(ren) _____

_____

Paint Easel	Blocks	Play House

Manipulatives	Crawling Area	Climbing Structure

Book Corner	Sensory Table	Rocking Chair

Appendix B: Professional Recommendations from the Field of Early Childhood Education

The National Association for the Education of Young Children, the largest professional organization for early educators, has long supported "developmentally appropriate" assessment of young children. In *Developmentally Appropriate Practice in Early Childhood Programs* (Bredekamp and Copple 1997, 21), the significant publication of the basic tenets of this organization, the authors state, "In developmentally appropriate programs, assessment and curriculum are integrated, with teachers continually engaging in observational assessment for the purposes of improving teaching and learning."

In 2003 the National Association for the Education of Young Children (NAEYC) and the National Association of Early Childhood Specialists in State Departments of Education (NAECS/SDE) adopted a position statement for Recommendations for Early Childhood Assessment. Throughout this position paper, information from the Chief Council of State School Officers is incorporated. The Key Recommendation of the position (2003, 10) states,

> *Make ethical, appropriate, valid, and reliable assessment a central part of all early childhood programs. To assess young children's strengths, progress, and needs, use assessment methods that are developmentally appropriate, culturally and linguistically responsive, tied to children's daily activities, supported by professional development, inclusive of families, and connected to specific, beneficial purposes: (1) making sound decisions about teaching and learning, (2) identifying significant concerns that may require focused intervention for individual children, and (3) helping programs improve their educational and developmental interventions. . . .*

Assessment methods include observation, documentation of children's work, checklists and rating scales, and portfolios, as well as norm-referenced tests. . . . In general, assessment specialists have urged great caution in the use and interpretation of standardized tests of young children's learning, especially in the absence of complimentary evidence when the stakes are potentially high.

These organizations (2003, 11) go on to identify the following Indicators of Effectiveness regarding assessment in the early childhood years:

- *Ethical principles guide assessment practices. . . . Young children are not denied opportunities or services, and decisions are not made about children on the basis of a single assessment.*
- *Assessment instruments are used for their intended purposes.*
- *Assessments are appropriate for the ages and other characteristics of children being assessed.*
- *Assessment instruments are in compliance with professional criteria for quality. . . . Assessments are valid and reliable.*
- *What is assessed is developmentally and educationally significant.*
- *Assessment evidence is used to understand and improve learning.*
- *Assessment evidence is gathered from realistic settings and situations that reflect children's actual performance.*
- *Assessments use multiple sources of evidence gathered over time.*
- *Screening is always linked to follow-up. . . . Diagnosis or labeling is never the result of a brief screening or one-time assessment.*
- *Use of individually administered, norm-referenced tests is limited.*
- *Staff and families are knowledgeable about assessment.*

In 2003 the Council for Chief State School Officers Early Childhood Education Assessment Panel produced a glossary of terms in order to clarify the meaning of various words used regarding the assessment of young children. "The Words We Use: A Glossary of Terms for Early Childhood Education Standards and Assessment" can be found at its Web site, www.ccsso.org. It defines assessment as "the gathering of information in order to make an evaluation." This gathering of information can take any of the following forms: observations, portfolios, interviews, projects, tests, and other resources. They offer the following clarifications of the terms "assessment," "evaluation," and "test":

- *Assessment is not a synonym for evaluation; assessment is gathering information; evaluation is making judgments about that information.*
- *"Assessment" and "test" are not synonymous. The results contribute to judgments made when assessing children and/or programs.*
- *The reliability and validity of assessments increase with children's age.*
- *Children younger than primary age have not attained the developmental capabilities to understand the purposes of formal testing. . . . There is wide agreement among researchers that the younger the child, the stronger the case for using more informal assessment processes.*

Here are the Council's definitions for these varying types of assessments, slightly adapted for use in this book. By distinguishing among these types, you can come to understand the value and importance of observational assessment as the most appropriate method for young children.

Test: One or more questions, problems, and/or tasks designed to estimate a child's knowledge, understanding, ability, skill, and/or attitudes in a consistent fashion for all individuals. Information from a test or tests contributes to judgments made in an assessment process.

Informal Assessment: A procedure for obtaining information that can be used to make judgments of children or programs using means other than standardized instruments; takes place on a continuous basis in everyday classroom conditions; can be used in consistent and valid ways.

Performance-based (Alternate, Alternative, Authentic) Assessment: Any assessment strategy designed to estimate a child's knowledge, understanding, ability, skill, and/or attitudes in a consistent fashion across individuals emphasizing methods other than standardized achievement tests, particularly those using multiple-choice formats; typically includes exhibitions, investigations, demonstrations, written or oral responses, journals, and portfolios. Children demonstrate knowledge and skills through a set of tasks. Describes accommodations made to enable children with disabilities to participate in the assessment process. Although these assessments are more time-consuming and costly to implement than paper-and-pencil assessments, many believe performance-based assessments give a more accurate, realistic, and culturally meaningful portrayal of children's capabilities.

Developmental Assessment: An ongoing process of observing a child's current competencies (including dispositions and attitudes) and using the information to help the child develop within the context of family and caregiving and learning environments; makes extensive use of observational assessment.

Observational Assessment: A process in which the teacher systematically observes and records information about the child's level of development and/or knowledge, skills, and attitudes in order to determine what has been learned, improve teaching, and support the child's progress. A checklist or notes are often used to record what has been observed. Effective observational assessment involves recording children's behavior at the time it occurs and training observers to be objective in recording behavioral descriptions. Many early childhood educators believe that observational assessment is the most valid form of assessment for use with young children because of their limitations to show what they know through conventional pencil-and-paper tests.

Here is a Glossary of Assessment Terms and Phrases from the position paper by NAEYC and NAECS/SDE (2003, 27–28). We include these here to support your efforts in following their recommendations and hope this will help in your learning process about using observation for assessment purposes.

Assessment: The process of obtaining information about a child in order to make judgments about their characteristics and decisions about appropriate teaching and care

Observational assessment: Assessment based on teachers' systematic recordings and analysis of children's behavior in real-life situations

Documentation: The process of keeping track of and preserving children's work as evidence of their progress

Child Development: The social, emotional, physical, and cognitive changes in children stimulated by biological maturation interacting with experience

Early Learning Standards: Statements that describe expectations for the learning and development of young children

Developmentally Appropriate: Practices that result from the process of professionals making decisions about the well-being and education of children based on at least three important kinds of information or knowledge: what is known about child development and learning . . . ; what is known about the strengths, interests, and needs of each individual child in the group . . . ; and knowledge of the social and cultural contexts in which children live

Criterion or Performance-Oriented Assessment: Assessment in which the person's performance (that is, score) is interpreted by comparing it with a prespecified standard or specific content and/or skills

Standardized: An assessment with clearly specified administration and scoring procedures and normative data

Norm-Referenced: A standardized testing instrument by which the person's performance is interpreted in relation to the performance of a group of peers who have previously taken the same test— a "norming" group

Reliability: The consistency of an assessment tool; important for generalizing about children's learning and development

Validity: The extent to which a measure or assessment tool measures what it was designed to measure

Screening: The use of a brief procedure or instrument designed to identify, from within a large population of children, those children who may need further assessment to verify developmental and/or health risks

References

- Bredekamp, Sue, and Carol Copple, editors. 1997. *Developmentally appropriate practice in early childhood.* Revised edition. Washington, D.C.: National Association for the Education of Young Children.

- Council for Chief State School Officers Early Childhood Education Assessment Panel. 2003. The words we use: A glossary of terms for early childhood education standards and assessment. http://www.ccsso.org.

- National Association for the Education of Young Children and National Association of Early Childhood Specialists in State Departments of Education. 2003. Early childhood curriculum, assessment, and program evaluation: Building an effective accountable system in programs for children birth through age 8. http://www.naeyc.org.

Appendix C: Using *Focused Observations* as a Training Tool

We have written this book as a practical explanation of observing children in all of its facets. We recognize that the professional recommendations from the field of early childhood education strongly support using observation for assessment and curriculum planning. And we know that early educators throughout the world are attempting to implement observation in a variety of early childhood settings. We wanted you as an instructor or staff development leader to be able to easily use the book and video to help you teach observation skills and support early educators as they learn to watch children in action.

In our experiences as consultants and college educators, we have seen that early educators benefit from practicing observation in order to do it better. We have learned that sharing multiple ways of documenting observations helps answer questions about time constraints. And we have seen that it takes time to try methods out, to watch children in action, and to learn more about specific assessment tools, before many early educators are ready to apply what they are learning to curriculum planning. We kept all of this in mind as we wrote the book and put the video vignettes together.

Practice Observations

This book and video are designed to go hand in hand so that information is coupled with practice and implementation. At the end of every chapter we suggest video vignettes and activities to illustrate the points of the chapter. The book can also be used without the video. The activities are adapted so that you can use them with the video or have teachers practice observation in their own work or family settings. The activities can be used in college coursework, staff development sessions, in-service workshops, and staff meetings.

Applying what is read, trying it out, analyzing what worked and didn't work, and reflecting on what was learned through the observation experience can be done with the video vignettes or in the students' own life settings. It's the practice that is the most important! Our suggestion is that participants read the chapter before viewing the vignettes or doing the practice observations. In this way they come to the practice exercises with basic knowledge, terminology, and suggestions to apply to the viewing.

For each activity we have identified a purpose related to the content in the chapter, a suggested video vignette or a situation to observe, the process for watching the child and documenting what is seen, and a focus for group discussion. The activities correlate with the order of the video vignettes from number one through number sixteen. However, you can use each practice observation in many different ways. Feel free to use them in any way that is most beneficial to your group or training situation. Watching the same video vignette more than once will increase understanding of how much can be learned through observation and give more in-depth knowledge of ways to interpret what is seen. In fact, you will see that we have repeated two of the vignettes about Christian toward the end of the video so that they can be viewed with a third one showing him involved in another activity. We suggest that you use these three vignettes to let teachers practice pulling information together and building a case about a child. We repeated them in a group of three so that it would be easy for you to show them to your students and staff members without having to rewind the videotape. At the end of this appendix we have included a list of the vignettes and their running times. This will help you plan your viewing sessions.

We suggest that the instructor or staff development leader view the video in its entirety first, looking over the suggested activities at the end of each chapter. In that way you can determine how best to make use of these tools. When you do this, please note that it was not designed to be used this way for training purposes. Instead, we included these features to make it easier to use one vignette at a time in a staff development session or a college class:

- Each vignette is numbered and a voice-over suggests viewing the vignette with a specific purpose in mind. This correlates to the suggestion in this book.
- A clock counts down ten seconds before the vignette actually begins.

- The children's names and ages are given in the video, as well as the activities in which they are involved.
- At the end of each vignette, the screen blacks out for a full ten seconds so that you have plenty of time to stop the tape and begin a discussion about what participants observed in the vignette.

Additional Activities

In addition to the video activities, two other types of activities are included at the end of each chapter:

- Reflection
- Finding Your Observation Style (a journaling activity)

The reflection activities are designed to help students and staff members think about the content of the chapter, analyzing and applying that content to their experiences with observing young children. The questions can be answered in writing as a formal assignment or can be used for discussion starters. The second set of activities, Finding Your Observation Style, is designed to be used in an ongoing journal format. We have learned that there are many right ways of using observation to take in information about children's growth and development. Each person implementing observation will bring to the task her own personality style, organizational and management tendencies, and understanding of child development. We hope the questions we ask and the personal journaling in response to those questions will help each individual recognize her own strengths and weaknesses in learning to implement this important task. We also hope that by the end of your experience with this book and video, you will have learned new techniques and determined more successful ways to implement observational assessment in the setting in which you work with children. Finally, we hope we have provided you with a helpful tool to plan for training and in-service sessions or coursework about observation!

Vignette 1:   *You may want to watch the following vignette to consider what can be learned by observing a child.*
   Daniel (4 yrs. 2 mos.), "Washing Hands and Snack"
   Running Time: 3 minutes 44 seconds

Vignette 2:   *You may want to watch the following vignette to consider factual versus interpretative documentation.*
   Alex (5 yrs. 1 mo.) and Matthew (4 yrs. 10 mos.), "Blocks"
   Running Time: 4 minutes 29 seconds

Vignette 3:   *You may want to watch the following vignette to consider factual versus interpretative documentation.*
Paris (5 yrs. 5 mos.), Kelsey (3 yrs. 10 mos.), and Keyonna (3 yrs. 5 mos.), "Dramatic Play"
Running Time: 6 minutes 28 seconds

Vignette 4:   *You may want to watch the following vignette to consider different ways to document observations.*
Christian (2 yrs. 7 mos.), "Making Music"
Running Time: 2 minutes 3 seconds

Vignette 5:   *You may want to watch the following vignette to consider different ways to document observations.*
Megan (4 yrs. 8 mos.), "Painting"
Running Time: 5 minutes 46 seconds

Vignette 6:   *You may want to watch the following vignette to consider different ways to document observations.*
Hunter (1 yr. 10 mos.), "A Toddler in Action"
Running Time: 4 minutes 43 seconds

Vignette 7:   *You may want to watch the following vignette to consider different ways to document observations.*
Tyler (4 yrs. 4 mos.), Malik (4 yrs. 5 mos.), and Dontasia (4 yrs. 1 mo.), "Three Young Writers"
Running Time: 2 minutes 2 seconds

Vignette 8:   *You may want to watch the following vignette to consider ways to document observations while observing a group of children.*
Anthony, Devaughn, Tyler, Malik, Dontasia, Kelsey, Keyonna, and Antonio, "Pancakes Story: A Group of 3–5 Year Olds"
Running Time: 8 minutes 7 seconds

Vignette 9:   *You may want to watch the following vignette to consider identifying children's developmental capabilities.*
Christian (2 yrs. 7 mos.), "Listening to a Story"
Running Time: 3 minutes

Vignette 10: You may want to watch the following vignette to consider
identifying children's developmental capabilities.

Sydney (4 yrs. 10 mos.) and Jaiden (5 yrs. 1 mo.), "Working
with a Puzzle"

Running Time: 3 minutes 3 seconds

Vignette 11: You may want to watch the following vignette to consider
planning curricular strategies.

Nate (3 yrs. 9 mos.), "Working with a Puzzle"

Running Time: 3 minutes 32 seconds

Vignette 12: You may want to watch the following vignette to consider
planning curricular strategies.

Elias (2 yrs. 1 mo.), "Tubes and Bottles"

Running Time: 2 minutes 41 seconds

Vignette 13: You may want to watch this and the following two vignettes
to consider pulling it all together and building a case about
a child.

Christian (2 yrs. 7 mos.), "Making Music"

Running Time: 2 minutes 3 seconds

Vignette 14: You may want to watch this vignette, the preceding one, and
the following one to consider pulling it all together and
building a case about a child.

Christian (2 yrs. 7 mos.), "Listening to a Story"

Running Time: 3 minutes

Vignette 15: You may want to watch this vignette and the two preceding
ones to consider pulling it all together and building a case
about a child.

Christian (2 yrs. 7 mos.), "Playdough, Cups, and Binoculars"

Running Time: 4 minutes 20 seconds

Vignette 16: You may want to watch the following vignette to consider
enjoying children and being in the moment with them.

Phoebe (3 yrs. 0 mos.), "Outdoors"

Running Time: 2 minutes 28 seconds

Index